Collins

Your Life

Student Book **4** New fully revised 3rd edition

The whole-school solution for Citizenship and PSHE

Now fully covering Economic Wellbeing and Financial Capability

John Foster,
Simon Foster and
Kim Richardson

Published by Collins
An imprint of HarperCollinsPublishers
77–85 Fulham Palace Road
Hammersmith
London
W6 8JB

Browse the complete Collins catalogue at
www.collinseducation.com

© HarperCollinsPublishers Limited 2010

10 9 8 7 6 5 4 3 2 1

ISBN 978-0-00-734518-2

John Foster, Simon Foster and Kim Richardson assert their moral right to be identified as the authors of this work.

British Library Cataloguing in Publication Data
A Catalogue record for this book is available from the British Library.

Commissioned by: Charlie Evans

Edited by Louise Wilson

Design by Jordan Publishing Design
Layout by Patricia Briggs

Cover design by Angela English

Printed in Spain by Gráficas Estella

Production by Simon Moore

Acknowledgements

The Publishers gratefully acknowledge the following for permission to reproduce copyright material. While every effort has been made to trace the copyright holders, in cases where this has been unsuccessful or if any have inadvertently been overlooked, the Publishers will be pleased to make the necessary arrangements at the first opportunity.

Text extracts: p. 6: 'Culture Club' by Dinah Starkey, from 'Respect', TES Supplement, 4 July 2003, pg 6. Copyright © Dinah Starkey 2003. Reprinted with the kind permission of the author; p. 9: 'Roots and Branches' by Nadia Marks, from The Guardian, 17 March, 2004. Copyright © Nadia Marks 2004. Reprinted with permission; p. 15: 'Growing up under the law' adapted from the FPI booklet 'Is it legal?' see further www.familyandparenting.org/bookshop; p. 25: 'Antisocial behaviour' adapted from www.direct.gov.uk, © Crown Copyright; p. 26: Extracts from 'The Youth Justice system' from the Youth Justice Board for England and Wales' website. Reprinted with permission; pp. 28–9: Extracts from 'Running a mock trial', from www.citizenshipfoundation.org.uk. Reprinted with permission; p. 29: Extracts from 'Barring the Way to Success' by Lucie Russell, from The Big Issue. 28 April–4 May 2003. Reprinted with permission; p. 49: 'Self-image' reproduced with permission from www.youth2youth.co.uk; p. 49: Extract about designer clothes by Wayne Hemmingway. Reprinted with the kind permission of the author; p. 50: 'Young, female and bankrupt' by Olinka Koster, from Daily Mail, 17 June 2009. Extract reprinted with permission of Solo Syndication; p. 50: 'PM Wants "Diversity" to be Youth Role Models', from Daily Star, 15 August 2009. Reprinted with permission; p. 50: Extracts slightly adapted from Sisters Unlimited by Jessica Howie, published by Vermilion. Used by permission of The Random House Group Limited; p. 51: Extracts from www.raisingkids.co.uk, reprinted with their kind permission; p. 51: Extracts from Being a Happy Teenager by Andrew Matthews. Copyright © Andrew Matthews. Reprinted with the kind permission of Seashell Publishers Pty Ltd, Australia; p. 53: Extracts from Being a Happy Teenager by Andrew Matthews. Copyright © Andrew Matthews. Reprinted with the kind permission of Seashell Publishers Pty Ltd, Australia; p. 54: 'How to be assertive without being aggressive' by Caro Handley; p. 55: Extracts from 'A quarrel a day...' from 19 magazine, March 2004, pg 28. Copyright © IPC Syndication/19. Some extracts in this article are taken from Make Love Work For You by Anne Nicholls, Piatkus. Extracts reprinted with permission of IPC Syndication and Piatkus; p. 56: Extract from Adolescence: The Survival Guide for Parents and Teenagers by E Fenwick and T Smith (Dorling Kindersley Revised Edition, 1998). Copyright © Dorling Kindersley 1998. Reprinted with permission of Penguin Group UK; p. 57: Extracts slightly adapted from Sisters Unlimited by Jessica Howie, published by Vermilion. Used by permission of The Random House Group Limited; p. 58: Extracts from Girls' Talk by Maria Pallotta-Chiarolli, published by Finch Publishing Pty Ltd, Australia, pp 61–3, 1998. Reprinted with the kind permission of the author; p. 59: Extract from Boys About Boys by Nick Fisher, published by Pan Macmillan 1991. Reprinted with permission of the publishers; p. 60: Extracts slightly adapted from Sisters Unlimited by Jessica Howie, published by Vermilion. Used by permission of The Random House Group Limited; p. 61: Extract from Tell It Like It Is by Katie Masters published by Virgin Books. Copyright © Katie Masters, 2002, Virgin Books Limited. Reprinted by permission of Virgin Books Ltd; p. 62: Extracts from www.childbereavement.org.uk. Reprinted with permission; p. 63: Extract taken from rd4u.org.uk reprinted with permission of Cruse Bereavement Care; p. 63: 'It happens to us all' extracts taken from 'The Issue: Bereavement', TES, 3 September 2002, pp 16–17. Reprinted with permission of TES; p. 64: 'Case study – Lisa's story' from www.leavinghome.info, the Scottish Council for Single Homeless (SCSH); p. 70: 'You and your body image – be realistic' reproduced from www.teenissues.co.uk; p. 70: 'A false picture' reproduced from www.kidsexercise.co.uk; p. 72: 'Teenagers "too idle" to bother with good food' by Rober Uhlig, Daily Telegraph, 14 October 2003. Copyright © Telegraph Media Group Limited, 2003. Reprinted with permission; p. 73: 'Put VAT on high-fat food, urges GP by David Derbyshire', Daily Telegraph, 10 June 2003. Copyright © Telegraph Media Group Limited, 2003. Reprinted with permission; p. 74: Extracts from But you Don't Understand Me by Elaine Sishton and Charlotte Russell, published by John Hunt Publishing Limited. Reprinted with permission; p. 75: Extracts from But you Don't Understand Me by Elaine Sishton and Charlotte Russell, published by John Hunt Publishing Limited. Reprinted with permission; p. 75: Extract from Sex Ed by Dr. Miriam Stoppard, published by Dorling Kindersley, © 1997 Dorling Kindersley, text copyright © 1997 by Miriam Stoppard. Reprinted by permission of Penguin Group UK; pp. 76–7: 'The low down on contraception' and 'The low down on pregnancy' taken from an article in J17, February 2004 entitled 'Let's Talk About Sex'. Reprinted by permission of Emap Elan Syndications; p. 77: 'I feel ashamed says Sophie 16' taken from an article in J17, February 2004 entitled 'Just Say No!'. Reprinted by permission of Emap Elan Syndications; p. 78: Extracts from XY–A Toolkit For Life by Matt Whyman, published by Hodder. Reprinted with permission of Hodder & Stoughton Limited; p. 79: 'Doctors vote to ban TV adverts "glorifying" drink by Celia Hall', Daily Telegraph, 3 July 2003. © Telegraph Media Group Limited, 2003. Reprinted with permission; p. 79: Extracts from XY–A Toolkit For Life by Matt Whyman, published by Hodder. Reprinted with permission of Hodder & Stoughton Limited; p. 80: Extracts from XY–A Toolkit For Life by Matt Whyman, published by Hodder. Reprinted with permission of Hodder & Stoughton Limited; pp. 86 and 87: Extracts from Connexions Step Two Booklet and Options at 16, © Crown Copyright; p. 92: 'School leavers can't budget, says research' by Rebecca Smithers, The Guardian, 29 April 2002. © The Guardian. Reprinted with permission; p. 94: Extract from Young Citizen's Passport, by Tony Thorpe, published by Hodder & Stoughton Educational. Copyright © the Citizenship Foundation 2003. Reprinted with permission of Hodder Arnold; p. 95: 'Why do I need a bank account' from www.fsa.go.uk.

Photos: p. 6: PA Photos; p. 8(x2): iStock; p. 9(x2): iStock; p. 10(b): iStock; p. 10(t): PA Photos; p. 11: Reuters Picture Library/Sebastian Derungs; p. 12: PA Photos; p. 13: iStock; p. 14: iStock; p. 15: Alamy/Chris Cooper-Smith; p. 16: iStock; p. 17: iStock; p. 19: iStock; p. 20: iStock; p. 21: © Lance Bellers/Fotolia.com; p. 23: Rex Features; p. 24: © Lance Bellers/Fotolia.com; p. 25: © Lance Bellers/Fotolia.com; p. 26(l): Telegraph Media Group; p. 26(r): Photoshot; p. 27(r): Corbis; p. 27(l): iStock; p. 29: PA Photos; p. 30: © moodboard/Fotolia.com; p. 31(x2): iStock; p. 32: Rex Features; p. 33: Corbis; p. 32: © jaddingt/Fotolia.com; p. 34: PA Photos; p. 35(x2): PA Photos; p. 37: Courtesy of Eastleigh Liberal Democrats; p. 38(x2): PA Photos; p. 39: PA Photos; p. 40: PA Photos; p. 41: PA Photos; p. 42(r): iStock; p. 42(l): Plain Stupid/Press Association Image; p. 43: Photofusion Photo Library; p. 44(x2): PA Photos; p. 45: PA Photos; p. 46: Alamy/Fresh Start Images; p. 48: iStock; p. 49: iStock; p. 50: Rex Features; p. 52: iStock; p. 53: iStock; p. 55: iStock; p. 56: Alamy/Catchlight Visual Services; p. 57: Alamy/Bubbles Picture Library; p. 59: iStock; p. 60: iStock; p. 61: iStock; p. 62: iStock; p. 63: iStock; p. 64: iStock; p. 66(x2): iStock; p. 68: iStock; p. 70(x2): PA Photos; p. 72: Alamy/Angela Hampton; p. 73: Alamy/Steve Stock; p. 74: iStock; p. 75: iStock; p. 76: iStock; p. 77: © moodboard/Fotolia.com; p. 78: Corbis; p. 80: iStock; p. 81: iStock; p. 84(x2): iStock; p. 85: iStock; p. 86: Photofusion Picture Library; p. 88(x2): iStock; p. 92: iStock; p. 94: © Kai Bialasiewicz/Fotolia.com; p. 95: iStock; p. 96: iStock; p. 98(l): Art Directors Photo Library; p. 99: Alamy/Art Directors Photo Library; p. 100: iStock; p. 101: © nextrecord/Fotolia.com; p. 102(b): Courtesy of Waldegrave School; p. 102(t): Chris Callow/AC Photography; p. 103(t): © Iaroslav Danylchenko/Fotolia.com; p. 103(b): Roger Scruton; p. 104: iStock; p. 105(r): © PictureArt/Fotolia.com; p. 105(tl): © Andrey Armyagov/Fotolia.com; p. 105(tr): © Alex Yeung/Fotolia.com; p. 105(l): © Sue Ashe/Fotolia.com.

Contents

Your Life 4 and Your Life 5 together form a comprehensive two-year course in Citizenship and Personal, Social, Health and Economic Education (PSHEE) at Key Stage 4. The table shows how the eight Citizenship units and thirteen PSHEE units cover the requirements of the National Curriculum Programme of Study for Citizenship and the frameworks for Personal wellbeing and Economic wellbeing and financial capability.

Citizenship

Developing as a citizen

These units aim to help you to understand how you can play a full part as a citizen in British society.

Unit 1 **Britain: a diverse society** (Citizenship 1.3a, 1.3b, 2.1a, 2.1b, 2.1c, 3l, 4j; Personal wellbeing 1.5a)

Unit 2 **Human rights** (Citizenship 1.2a, 1.2b, 1.2c, 2.1a, 2.1b, 2.1c, 3a, 3f)

Unit 3 **Rights and responsibilities** (Citizenship 1.2a, 1.2b, 2.1a, 2.1b, 2.1c, 3k; Economic wellbeing and financial capability 1.2d, 3a, 3c)

Unit 4 **The law of the land** (Citizenship 1.1b, 2.1a, 3b, 3c)

Unit 5 **Crime and punishment** (Citizenship 1.1b, 2.1a, 2.1b, 2.2a, 2.2b, 2.2c, 3b, 3c)

Unit 6 **It's your government** (Citizenship 1.1a, 1.1d, 2.1a, 3c, 3d, 3e, 4a)

Unit 7 **It's your council** (Citizenship 1.1a, 2.1a, 2.1d, 3d, 4a, 4b)

Unit 8 **Working for change** (Citizenship 1.1a, 2.3a, 2.3b, 2.3c, 2.3d, 2.3e, 3d, 3g, 3h, 4a, 4b, 4c, 4d, 4e; Economic wellbeing and financial capability 4a)

Personal, Social, Health and Economic Education

Personal wellbeing – Understanding yourself and handling relationships

These units concentrate on developing your self-knowledge and your ability to manage your emotions and handle your relationships

Unit 9 Developing your identity and image (Personal wellbeing 1.1a, 1.1b, 1.2a, 1.2c, 2.1a)

Unit 10 Managing your emotions and moods (Personal wellbeing 1.4a, 1.4c, 2.1b, 2.1d, 2.1e, 2.2e, 2.3a, 2.3b)

Unit 11 Changing relationships (Personal wellbeing 1.1c, 1.4a, 1.4c, 2.1d, 2.1e, 2.3a, 2.3b, 3f, 3g)

Unit 12 Coping with crises (Personal wellbeing 1.2a, 1.3a, 2.1d, 2.2a, 2.3e, 3i)

Unit 13 Challenging offensive behaviour (Personal wellbeing 1.5a, 1.5b, 2.1a, 2.3d, 3a, 3j; Citizenship 1.1c, 1.2a, 1.2b, 2.1a, 4a)

Personal wellbeing – Keeping healthy

These units are designed to help you to understand how to develop a healthy, safer lifestyle, to think about the alternatives when making decisions about personal health, and the consequences of such decisions.

Unit 14 Healthy eating (Personal wellbeing 1.2a, 1.2b, 2.2a, 3b, 3d)

Unit 15 Safer sex and contraception (Personal wellbeing 1.2a, 1.3a, 1.3b, 1.3c, 2.2a, 2.2b, 2.2c, 3d, 3e)

Unit 16 Drinking and smoking (Personal wellbeing 1.2a, 1.3a, 1.3b, 2.2a, 2.2b, 2.2c, 2.2d, 3d, 3e)

Unit 17 Health matters (Personal wellbeing 1.2a, 1.2b, 1.3a, 2.2a, 2.2b, 2.2c, 3d, 3e, 4h)

Economic wellbeing and financial capability

The aim of these units is to develop your understanding of the world of work through undertaking an enterprise challenge and exploring how businesses are financed, to think about career opportunities and to learn about how to manage your money.

Unit 18 Thinking ahead – planning your future (Economic wellbeing and financial capability 1.1a, 1.1b, 1.1c, 2.1a, 2.1b, 2.1c, 2.1d, 2.2a, 2.3a, 2.3c, 3c, 3e, 3f, 4a, 4b, 4c, 4d, 4f, 4h)

Unit 19 Managing your money (Economic wellbeing and financial capability 1.2b, 2.4a, 2.4b, 2.4c, 2.4d, 3h)

Unit 20 Financing businesses (Economic wellbeing and financial capability 1.3a, 1.3b, 1.4a, 1.4b, 2.3i, 3g, 3j, 4a, 4g)

Unit 21 Enterprise challenge (Economic wellbeing and financial capability 1.2a, 1.4,a 2.3f, 2.3g, 2.3h, 3g, 4a, 4c, 4f, 4g, 4h)

Reviewing

This unit provides a framework for assessing the knowledge, skills and understanding developed in Citizenship and Personal, Social, Health and Economic Education during the course.

Unit 22 Reviewing and recording your learning

CULTURE CLUB

The English nation has been made as a result of migration – and is all the better for it, says Dinah Starkey

Aim To explore the origins of Britain as a multicultural and multiethnic society, and the benefits that this has brought (Citizenship 1.3a, 1.3b, 2.2a, 2.2b, 2.2c, 3l, 4j; Personal wellbeing 1.5a)

The English are the product of centuries of migration, some peaceful, some forcible. John Bull, the typical Englishman, may in fact be two parts Germanic Saxon to one part Celt, with a chunk of Scandinavian, a smattering of French and a dash of West Indian, Asian, Jewish or Irish. The asylum seekers who enter our country today are only the latest immigrants.

Scotland and Wales have had their newcomers too, but England has always been a bigger melting pot. The Scots and the Welsh kept their native languages and culture for much longer, and even now they have a separate identity.

Go back 40,000 years and the original ancient Britons were arriving from continental Europe. They were followed, much later, by the Beaker people, who brought with them skills in working the mysterious new metal – bronze.

The Celts arrived about 700BC, and with them came the Iron Age. Next were the Romans in 43AD. They stayed for nearly 400 years, transforming the landscape with road systems, farming methods and new crops. Many of the towns they established still survive.

By 410AD the Roman empire was crumbling, and the Angles and Saxons began to raid across the sea from what is now Germany. It was the Saxons who named the shires and villages, and the English language began to take shape. The Normans, themselves the descendants of the Vikings, held all

things Saxon in contempt and invaded in 1066. They ignored the native language and continued to speak Norman French for generations. But the locals went on using Saxon, and gradually the two languages began to merge.

As trade routes opened in Tudor times, African boys were brought to Britain to satisfy the fashionable demand for black servants called blackamoors. By the end of Queen Elizabeth I's reign in 1603, an estimated 20,000 'blackamoors' were living and working in London.

The Huguenots, a French Protestant group, flooded into Britain in the 17th century to escape persecution by Catholic France. Many were cloth workers and they brought with them techniques which revitalised the British textile industry. In the 19th century, tens of thousands of Irish immigrants came to England after the potato famine, and from 1881 mounting persecution in Eastern Europe and Russia led to the arrival of thousands of Jews.

The evolution of the British national identity has been slow and painful. The struggle for success that has faced each generation of immigrants continues today. Perhaps we can help to make the process of assimilation a little easier by teaching young people about their past. That way they may come to understand what incomers have brought to our country and what they might contribute in the centuries to come.

Source: *TES Supplement*

In groups

1 Why could England be described as a 'melting pot'?

2 Identify three different reasons why immigrant groups have come to Britain in the last 40,000 years. Are these the same reasons why different peoples are still coming to Britain today?

3 Why is this ethnic immigration described as 'Britain's benefit'?

4 Discuss why you think people coming to Britain are often met with hostility and resentment.

Britain's benefit

Britain has benefited from ethnic diversity throughout its history. From industry and commerce to art and dance, from sport and music to science and literature, the activities of individuals and groups from ethnic minorities have enriched life in Britain for all.

Newcomers have often met hostility and resentment, yet even a quick study would show that they have brought skills and qualifications, set up businesses and created jobs, not only for themselves but also for local people. Many have been willing to do jobs that local people have been unwilling to do.

What is remarkable and often not understood is that the contributions immigrants and their immediate descendants have made – and continue to make – to Britain are out of all proportion to their numbers.

Source: www.cre.org.uk/ethdiv

Immigration into Britain:
the last 60 years

1948	The first West Indian immigrants come to Britain, invited by the British government to help address the shortage of unskilled workers.
1960	India and Pakistan begin to issue passports to allow economic migration to Britain. In 1961, 48,850 people arrive from these countries.
1968–76	Thousands of African Asians come from East Africa, many to escape the persecution of the dictator Idi Amin. Many bring useful business and professional skills.
1976	The Race Relations Act is passed to promote racial equality and tackle discrimination. The Commission for Racial Equality is set up.
1979	The first of 22,000 Vietnamese refugees arrive, fleeing Communism in Vietnam.
1992	The Maastricht Treaty is passed, allowing citizens of the European Union states to live and work in Britain.
2003	Asylum seekers continue to seek a haven in Britain from persecution and war in countries such as Sri Lanka, Iraq and Afghanistan.
2004	The expansion of the European Union brings an influx of workers from eastern European countries, such as Poland.

In groups

1 Study the timeline 'Immigration into Britain'. What do you learn from it about the main groups of immigrants that have come to Britain in the last 60 years?

2 Use the information on these pages to extend this timeline backwards 40,000 years. Call it 'The Making of Britain'.

On your own

On your own, choose one of the immigrant groups mentioned in the articles and find out more about their history. What reasons did they have for coming, and what have they contributed to Britain's culture?

Is there a national identity and culture in Britain?

Aim To explore the meaning of national identity and culture (Citizenship 1.3a, 1.3b, 2.1a, 2.1b, 2.1c, 3l; Personal wellbeing 1.5a)

What does 'being British' mean?

The British Citizenship test

Since 2005, people who want to become British citizens have had to take the British Citizenship test. It was introduced to ensure that they know about the country they are adopting, and understand what it means to be a part of British society.

The test is also required if you want indefinite leave to remain in the UK (otherwise known as naturalisation).

The test takes 45 minutes and consists of 24 questions about life in the UK, focusing on its history, society and culture. The test has to be taken at an approved centre.

All applicants are given a booklet called Life in the UK so that they can prepare for the test, and there are practice questions and other advice on the Immigration Office website. As the test is in English, applicants have to make sure that their level of English is good enough. This may mean attending an English course.

Applicants have to get 75 per cent to pass the test. It can be retaken if necessary. Those who are successful are given a letter as proof of passing. They cannot apply for citizenship without this letter.

The citizenship ceremony

Those whose application for citizenship has been approved are invited to attend a citizenship ceremony. At these ceremonies groups of new citizens are welcomed – both into British citizenship and into the local community.

The ceremony stresses the fact that becoming a citizen carries with it both rights and responsibilities. It encourages new citizens to play an active part in the community. Usually the mayor and other local officials attend the ceremony to reinforce this message.

For your file

Read about the British Citizenship test. Write your views on whether or not you think this is a good idea.

"You're only truly British if you were born in Britain."

"It means having a passport as a British citizen."

"It means speaking English and accepting the British way of life."

"It's got nothing to do with race or religion or cultural traditions. All sorts of people are British, because their families have chosen to live here."

"You're British if you've made your permanent home in the UK."

In pairs

Read what these young people have to say about being British. Discuss what being British means to you.

Roots and branches

How do ethnic minority families manage to retain their heritage while living in Britain? Nadia Marks talks to two families with roots abroad:

Sunil and Parul Shah are Hindu, live in Milton Keynes and have two sons, Mayur, 14, and Tushar, 16

SUNIL: "My father emigrated from India to Africa, where I was born, and so did my wife's parents. Our parents managed to keep their ethnic identity and pass it on to us, so we are passing it on to our children. Our culture, language, religion and moral values are all important in identifying who, and what, we are.

It was important for us to marry a Hindu because we have the same values and are raising our children in agreement. But we understand the importance of adapting to western culture."

MAYUR: "When I was small I used to be embarrassed if my parents spoke to me in Gujarati, but now I am proud and very pleased to be able to communicate with my grandmother, who doesn't speak English. It gives me a sense of my culture and reminds me of who I am."

Roya and Hossein Shahidi are Iranians who live in London. They have two sons, Farhang, 15, and Farhad, 21

ROYA: "You cannot get away from who you are culturally, but given the choice you can create your own unique culture and be a more enriched person. We are Persian-Iranian and have a rich culture, such as our language, history, literature, music and food. These are all things we want to pass down to our children. I feel it is a blessing to be able to embrace two cultures, and it is beneficial not only to us as immigrants but to our host country, too. It is a two-way process."

FARHANG: "Being Iranian is not something that I consciously think about. I suppose I feel as British as I do Iranian because I fit into both cultures with the same ease. What does make me feel good, though, is the knowledge that I have this dual nationality. I know what it is like to be a foreigner in this country, but I also know what it is like being British."

In groups

1 Discuss what the families on the left are saying about being part of more than one culture.

2 Do they identify with one culture more than the other?

3 Are the conflicting loyalties a burden or a benefit?

4 Do the children feel any differently from their parents?

In pairs

"I'm a British African-Caribbean. My parents came to Britain from the West Indies before I was born. They're British West Indians."

"I'm from Glasgow. I'm Scottish and British."

"My parents are from Pakistan. I'm from Oldham. I suppose I'm a Lancastrian British Asian."

Discuss what you think these young people are saying about their identity. How would you describe your own identity, and that of your family?

Source: 'Roots And Branches' by Nadia Marks, *The Guardian*

What are human rights?

Human rights are ideas about what everyone is entitled to. Basic human rights include the right to life, and the right to food and clean drinking water. Others include the right to vote and to freedom of expression.

In the UK, most people have their basic human rights met most of the time. However, in some countries people's freedoms may be limited. Also, in the UK, there are still areas of human rights that some people believe could be improved, such as the rights of people with disabilities (see page 13).

Aim To discuss what human rights are and which rights are most important (Citizenship 1.2a, 1.2b, 1.2c, 2.1a, 2.1b, 2.1c, 3a, 3f)

88 In groups

Look at the photo on the left of protesters clashing with riot police outside the Bank of England in London. Do you think that human rights are being violated here? If so, which ones?

Where did human rights come from?

The modern idea of human rights was developed after the Second World War, during which many people's rights were violated. On a large scale, these human rights abuses are known as war crimes.

As a result, the United Nations (UN) was formed to provide a place for nations to resolve conflicts peacefully. It was set up by the Universal Declaration of Human Rights (UDHR), which consisted of 30 articles describing the basic rights of every person, and was signed in 1948 by 48 countries.

The first section of the Universal Declaration states:

"All human beings are born free and equal in dignity and rights."

Key rights relating to being "born free" include freedom of speech and of movement, the right to a fair trial, and freedom from torture and from hunger.

Key rights relating to "being equal" include a right to an education, and the right to be treated equally, without discrimination, in all areas of public life.

The Universal Declaration was designed as a safeguard to protect the human rights of people around the world. However, it has been criticised for being too weak because, as it is only a declaration, it cannot be enforced by law.

Human rights issues

A legal basis for human rights

The European Convention of Human Rights was introduced in 1953, giving a legal framework for human rights in the UK and other European countries. Here, people can complain to the European Court of Human Rights (or ECHR), based in Strasbourg, France.

In 1998, the European Union (EU) decided to update the list of human rights, to take account of changes in society and technology. The result was the European Charter of Fundamental Rights (2000). This included some newer human rights:

- The right to a private life, including a right to privacy and to confidentiality of letters and emails.

- The right to limits on working hours and to have annual paid holiday.

- The right to respect the integrity of human beings, including a ban on financial gain from the human body. This includes the sale of human organs and the cloning of human beings.

- The right to data protection, which means that if a company holds data on you, you can ask where it got the information and what it is.

The controversial Dignitas Clinic in Switzerland, which, by the beginning of 2009, had helped over 100 UK citizens to die.

In the UK, it has been against the law since 1961 for a person to help someone commit suicide. However, some campaigners have argued that this law is out of date. They argue that people who are terminally ill and want to commit suicide should have freedom of expression. Also, they argue that their families and friends should be able to help them travel to countries like Switzerland, where assisted suicide is legal.

However, other campaigners, including many religious groups, have reacted strongly against this. They argue that life is sacred, as made clear in the "right to life" section of the Universal Declaration of Human Rights. Here, it is argued that the right to life supersedes the right to freedom of expression, and you should not be allowed to commit suicide, or aid someone to do so, even if they are terminally ill.

Other campaigners argue that assisted suicide is hypocritical without a death penalty in the UK. Surely, if people are allowed to help or commit suicide when they are terminally ill, then shouldn't the state use the death penalty against murderers? If you can take life if you are terminally ill, shouldn't the state be able to take a life as a punishment?

In both the United States and China, the death penalty, or capital punishment is used as a means of punishment for severe crimes, such as murder. However, in the UK, the Government has argued that the "right to life" applies here. This is despite a majority of the UK population being consistently in favour of capital punishment in opinion polls.

For your file

If you could make one new law to enforce a human right, what right would you choose and why?

"I would create a law outlawing abortion in the UK. Everyone's entitled to the right to life."

"I would create a law making it free for everyone to go to University. Education should be a right, not a privilege."

In groups

Discuss what you think about the law on assisted suicide. Should it be changed for cases of terminal illness? Why? Give reasons for your views.

In groups

Do you think the UK ought to have capital punishment? Should the will of the majority be followed, even if it goes against majority rights? Give reasons for your views.

What are responsibilities?

Aim To discuss what responsibilities are and how they relate to human rights (Citizenship 1.2a, 1.2b, 1.2c, 2.1a 2.1b, 2.1c, 3a, 3f)

Responsibilities are necessary for people to protect each other's human rights. For example, you have the right to drive a car to increase your freedom of movement. However, you also have the responsibility to drive safely and to obey the Highway Code.

How **rights** become **responsibilities**

The table shows three articles from the Universal Declaration of Human Rights (UDHR) and their key responsibilities:

Human rights	Key responsibilities
Everyone should be treated in the same way, and laws should apply equally to everyone (Article 7).	We should treat everyone equally, whatever their age, gender, race or religion.
Everyone is innocent until it can be proven that they are guilty. Everyone has the right to defend themselves at any public trial. (Article 11).	We must listen to both sides of an argument and not jump to conclusions. People should have a chance to explain themselves.
Everyone is entitled to privacy (Article 12).	You should respect other people's privacy and they should respect yours. No one may enter your house or read your mail without good reason.

In pairs

Look at the table on the left. Which do you think are the most important rights and responsibilities? Why?

In groups

Do you think that Nick Griffin should have freedom of speech? Or should he be banned from public speaking because of his extreme views?

"I disagree with Nick Griffin. But people in the North-west of the UK elected him. Therefore, he should be allowed to express his views." Shona, Manchester

"The BNP has been accused of encouraging racial violence. I have the right to live peacefully. Therefore Nick Griffin should be banned from public events."
Tariq, Birmingham

Freedom of speech
– a conflict of rights?

In June 2009, Nick Griffin of the British National Party was elected MEP for the North-west region. The BNP, a whites-only party, has a series of policies which some campaigners believe to be racist. As a result, groups such as the Anti-Nazi league believe that Nick Griffin should be banned from speaking at public events. They argue that the BNP's racist ideas go against Article 7 of the UDHR, which states that "everyone has the right to be treated equally".

After being elected, Nick Griffin tried to give a press conference outside Parliament. However, he was heckled by anti-fascist demonstrators and pelted with eggs. Nick Griffin MEP argues that he has a "right to freedom of speech" as outlined in Article 19 of the Universal Declaration of Human Rights.

In July 2009, the Equality Commission wrote to the BNP to clarify its policy of having only white members. The Commission said that this went against the Human Rights Act, which states that people should have "freedom of association" and thus be able to join any political party they like, without discrimination. The BNP denied it was breaking any laws.

▶ BNP leader, Nick Griffin

Equal opportunities

In order to achieve Article 8 of the UDHR, the UK government promotes the idea of equal opportunities. This means that everyone has an equal opportunity in life, including in employment, education and access to services.

Disability rights in the UK

A disability is an impairment or medical condition that prevents someone from doing something. Physical impairments include hearing difficulties, vision impairment or mobility problems, such as being unable to walk without assistance. Other impairments, such as learning difficulties, restrict a person's mental development.

A wide variety of human rights exist to protect people with disabilities. Article 22 of the UDHR states that "Everyone, as a member of society, is entitled to realisation of their economic, social and cultural rights." This means that we, as individuals and as a society, have a responsibility to help people with disabilities lead as normal a life as possible.

The Disability Discrimination Act 1995

This Act means that everyone has the responsibility not to discriminate against people with disabilities with regard to:

- access to goods, facilities and services.
- employment
- the management, buying or renting of land or property.

From 2004, businesses have had to make reasonable changes to their properties to accommodate people with disabilities including:

- access ramps for people in wheelchairs.
- hearing loops for those who find it difficult to hear.
- colour-coding in large buildings, such as hospitals, for people whose vision is impaired.

In groups

Do you think public money should be spent on improving disabled access? Or is the money better spent on other projects? Give reasons for your views.

"The law says 'reasonable changes'. But a person shouldn't have to put a ramp in their shop. If there's a small kerb, so what?" Kyle, Norwich

"Disabled people should be treated equally and fairly – no more, no less." Anna, Plymouth

"I think more public money should be spent on improving disabled access. You only have to look down a street to see how difficult life could be if you were in a wheelchair. Or try closing your eyes and imagine what it would be like to have impaired vision." Nazma, Bradford

Parental responsibility

'Parental responsibility' is the phrase we use for the rights and responsibilities that parents have towards their children. Until a child reaches 16, its parents are responsible for:

- looking after them
- feeding and clothing them
- making decisions about their schooling
- agreeing to medical treatment
- making decisions about where they should live.

Although the Children Act (1989) defined the idea of parental responsibility, it only gives general guidelines – that parents must protect under-16s from harm. But what is harmful? That is a matter for the parent's judgement. Social services would get involved only if they felt that a child was at risk of suffering 'significant harm'.

Parents should make their decisions based on the age, maturity and wishes of a child. As Kay Macfarlane of the Scottish Child Law Centre says: "The key consideration when deciding to leave a child alone is whether you feel they are mature enough to know what to do in an emergency, such as a fire, and to follow your instructions if, say, someone comes to the door."

Aim To explore the rights and responsibilities of people at home and at school (Citizenship 1.2a, 1.2b, 2.1a, 2.1b)

In groups

1 Discuss parental responsibilities. Is it a good idea that the law leaves so much to the judgement of parents?

2 If the law laid down strict ages for leaving children on their own, what ages would you give?

3 There is no law that states the age at which young people can babysit, but child charities recommend that the minimum age of a babysitter should be 16. Do you agree? Would you want to take any other factors into consideration?

In pairs

Which are the two most important rights and the two most important responsibilities listed in the table below?

Rights and responsibilities at school

	Rights	Responsibilities
PARENTS	• To choose a school for their child • To educate their child out of school	• To ensure their child goes to school • To ensure their child is suitably educated between the ages of 5 and 16
STUDENTS	• To leave school at 16 • To be educated until they are 18	• To obey school rules • To behave sensibly and reasonably
TEACHERS	• To punish students, if there is reasonable cause • To confiscate certain items from students, e.g. drugs	• To look after the students in their care as if they were their parents
SCHOOLS	• To insist students wear a reasonable uniform • As a last resort, to exclude students for bad behaviour	• To take steps to prevent bullying • To provide students with religious and sex education

Growing up under the law

As you grow up, your right to do things varies according to how old you are. It also depends on what you want to do. Here are some different areas:

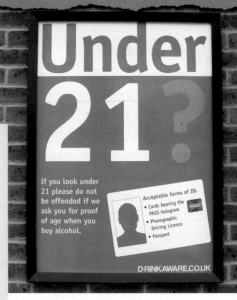

Under 21?

If you look under 21 please do not be offended if we ask you for proof of age when you buy alcohol.

Acceptable forms of ID:
• Cards bearing the PASS hologram
• Photographic Driving Licence
• Passport

DRINKAWARE.CO.UK

● Smoking and buying cigarettes

It is illegal to buy cigarettes if you are under 18. It is also illegal for shops to sell cigarettes to anyone under 18.

● Buying and using drugs

Children can be arrested and charged with possession of drugs, or with supplying drugs, from the age of 10.

● Going to the pub and drinking

Children under 14 can be refused entry to a bar. Children cannot buy and drink alcohol in a bar until they are 18. However, children can drink alcohol at home with their parents' permission from the age of 5.

● Gambling

You have to be 18 before you can legally enter a betting shop. You have to be 16 before you can buy a lottery ticket.

● Sexual relationships

The age of consent for sexual relationships is 16. This means that it is illegal for anyone to have penetrative sex under the age of 16, and also to indulge in forms of intimate sexual touching.

● Tattooing

You cannot get a tattoo until you reach the age of 18, except for medical reasons.

● Contraception

Young people can obtain contraceptive advice and treatment without their parents' consent. Doctors can provide advice and treatment to under-16s if they believe patients have sufficient maturity and understand the advice.

● Marriage

A young person can get married at 16 with the consent of his or her parents. Once a person reaches the age of 18, they can get married without their parents' consent.

● Learning to drive

A young person can obtain a licence for a moped from the age of 16, and for a motorbike from the age of 17. A young person can get a provisional driving licence for a car from the age of 17.

● Representation

You can vote and stand to be a Councillor or MP from the age of 18.

In pairs

1 Draw a timeline from 0 to 21 and mark on it at what age it is legal to do the various things listed on the left.

2 Research the age restrictions of some of the activities that have not been included, such as joining the armed forces, driving a heavy goods vehicle, buying a pet, or moving away from home. Add them to your timeline.

For your file

Are there any entries in your timeline that you disagree with? Choose one or more and write a paragraph explaining what the law is on these issues, why you think the law has been passed, and what your objections to it are.

Source: adapted from the FPI booklet *Is it legal?* www.familyandparenting.org

What is work?

Although most workers are employed on a full-time basis, there are many different patterns of work. There are permanent and temporary jobs. Part-time work has increased, with nearly as many women working part-time as are working full-time. Or people choose to be self-employed, which means they do not have an employer, but sell their labour directly to the customer. This can mean hard work and long hours, but the possibility of greater freedom by working independently.

As a result of modern technology, more office jobs are being done at home. There is also voluntary work – people working in the community for charities, hospitals and schools, etc. These volunteers earn no money but improve the quality of other people's lives. This is the same for unpaid work in the home, such as caring, cooking and housework.

In pairs

Discuss what counts as work in today's society. Write down one example of each of the different types of work listed above. What are the advantages and disadvantages of each? What is their value to society?

Aim To explore the rights and responsibilities of people at work (Citizenship 1.2a, 1.2b, 2.1a, 2.1b, 2.1c, 3k; Economic wellbeing and financial capability 3a, 3c)

Starting work

If you are employed for more than a month, you must have a contract with your employer. The contract lists the terms and conditions of employment. This includes your responsibilities, as well as your right to pay, holidays, etc. The contract can be agreed verbally, but employees have the right to a written statement of the main terms of employment within two months of starting work. This statement should give:

- Your job title and place of work.
- Your starting date.
- Details of how much you will be paid, and when
- Your hours of work
- Your holiday entitlement
- Arrangements for sick pay and pension
- Details of how complaints at work are dealt with
- The amount of notice you and your employer must give to end the contract.

For your file

A friend has e-mailed to say that she has started a new job, but has not received a contract. Reply to her explaining why you think it is important for her to have a contract. Add what you think the contract should include.

The law at work

There are a number of laws that protect the rights of employees and ensure equal opportunities at work. Here are five of the most important:

Equal Pay Act 1970

States that men and women should be paid the same. This covers all types of pay and reward, e.g. bonuses.

Health and Safety Act 1974

Employers have a legal duty to take care of their staff.

Sex discrimination Act 1975 and 1986

It is unlawful to discriminate against someone because of their sex.

Race Relations Act 1976

It is unlawful to discriminate against someone because of their race, colour, country of origin, nationality or ethnic group.

Disability Discrimination Act 1995

It is unlawful to discriminate against someone in terms of pay, promotion or other terms of employment at work because of a disability.

In pairs

"There are too many laws about employment and discrimination. Employers should be able to employ who they like and pay them what they like without fear of being accused of discrimination."

1 Discuss this view.

2 With a partner, imagine a situation where one of these laws has been broken. Role-play a scene in which one of you explains how they have been the victim of discrimination and asks for advice on what action to take.

Tribunals

Many disputes in the workplace go to an employment tribunal. This is a kind of court which hears both the employer's and employee's side of the argument. If the employee wins the case, they are usually awarded a sum of money (called compensation).

Case study

Sadie Frost's fashion boutique FrostFrench was ordered to pay £5000 to an employee who claimed she was discriminated against because of the colour of her skin. Aba Yankah said that while the store manager had been friendly to her over the phone, she was cold and distant when she met her in person and soon dismissed her.

For your file

Search the Internet to find examples of other cases of discrimination which have been taken to employment tribunals. Which type of discrimination appears to be the most common? Write a brief statement for your folder about discrimination in the workplace.

Consumers and traders

Aim To explore your rights and responsibilities as a consumer (Citizenship 1.2a, 1.2b, 2.1a, 2.1b, 3k; Economic wellbeing and financial capability 1.2d)

Your rights when shopping

Consumers may be shopping for goods (i.e. buying items) or for services (i.e. buying a skill such as a haircut or professional advice from a plumber). Either way they make a contract with the trader, which is legally binding in civil law (see page 20). If the goods or services supplied are faulty or inadequate, your rights are protected by law.

When buying goods...

Under the Sale of Goods Act, the law states that the goods must be:

- **of satisfactory quality** – taking into account the description and price
- **fit for their purpose** – they must do what the seller and manufacturer says they can do
- **as described** – they must fit the description on the package or display sign, or that given by the seller.

This law applies also to second-hand goods, and goods bought in a sale or by mail order, over the phone or on the Internet. It does not apply to goods bought privately. In this case, the seller must not mislead you and must describe the goods correctly.

When buying a service...

Under the Supply of Goods and Services Act, a service must be provided:

- **with reasonable care and skill** – the job should be done to a proper standard of workmanship
- **within a reasonable time** – even if you haven't agreed a definite completion date with the supplier of the service
- **for a reasonable charge** – unless you agreed a price beforehand. (An 'estimate' tells you roughly what the cost will be. A 'quotation' tells you the exact price and is part of the contract between you and the supplier.) 'Reasonable' means compared with the normal standard, e.g. what you would normally expect from a plumber, etc.

Civil and criminal laws

The Sale of Goods Act and the Supply of Goods and Services Act are civil laws. There are also some criminal laws that protect the consumer.

- **The Trades Description Act** says that it is illegal to give a false description of goods or services.

- **The Consumer Protection Act** says that it is illegal to sell unsafe goods or to mislead consumers about the price of goods. The manufacturer or importer is liable for any loss or damage caused.

- **The Food Safety Act** says that it is illegal to sell food that doesn't comply with food safety requirements.

For your file

The Ethical Consumer is a consumer organisation that investigates the social and environmental records of big brand names, and advises consumers to 'buy ethically'. Investigate one of the companies listed on www.ethicalconsumer.org and write a paragraph explaining why it is an ethical company to buy from.

When you have a complaint

Take the faulty item back to the shop as soon as possible and ask, firmly but politely, for a refund or for it to be exchanged. But what if the trader keeps arguing – what are your rights?

It isn't our fault the goods are defective – go back to the manufacturer.

NOT TRUE – *you bought the goods from the trader, not the manufacturer, and the trader is liable for any breaches of contract.*

You must produce your receipt.

NOT TRUE – *in fact, the trader doesn't have to give you a receipt in the first place. However, it might be reasonable for the shop to want some proof of purchase, such as a credit card receipt or bank statement.*

We don't give any refunds – you must accept a credit note.

IT DEPENDS. *If you have changed your mind, the shop doesn't have to do anything. But if the goods are faulty, incorrectly described or not fit for their normal purpose, you are entitled to your money back.*

No refunds can be given on sale items.

IT DEPENDS *on why you want to return them. The Sale of Goods Act still applies, but you won't be entitled to anything if you knew of any faults before purchase, if the fault should have been obvious to you, or if you simply changed your mind.*

You have rights for only 30 days after the date of purchase.

NOT TRUE – *depending on circumstances. You might be too late to have all your money back after this time, but the trader will still be liable for any breaches of contract, such as the goods being faulty.*

When are you *not* entitled to anything?

- If you were told of any faults before you bought the goods.
- If the fault was obvious and you should have noticed it before buying.
- If you caused any damage yourself.
- If you made a mistake, e.g. about the colour/size.
- If you have changed your mind about the goods or you have seen them cheaper elsewhere.
- If you bought the goods more than six years ago.

Source: adapted from
www.tradingstandards.gov.uk

In groups

1 Discuss your rights under the Sale of Goods Act. Draw up two lists – one stating when you are entitled to a refund or an exchange, and one stating when you are not entitled to anything.

2 Discuss your rights under the Supply of Goods and Services Act.

4 The law of the land

What is the law?

In an ideal world we would act exactly as we pleased. Unfortunately, many of the things we want to do clash with, or affect, other people. Societies have therefore developed complex systems of regulating (or controlling) people's behaviour.

Here's the deal: the law restricts your behaviour in return for protecting you. It imposes 'responsibilities' because it demands that you behave in a certain way. But it also provides you with 'rights': you will be backed up by the State if these rights are infringed by others.

Aim To understand what the law is and how laws are made (Citizenship 1.1b, 2.1a, 3b, 3c)

Laws in the UK

Law

A set of rules that regulate the relationships between people, between states, and between the people and the state. These rules are enforceable in the courts.

International law

Aimed at settling disputes between nations over such things as where they can trade or what weapons they can have. International law comes from treaties agreed between nations.

National law

The law that applies within a particular country. Laws passed by the British Parliament apply to the whole of the UK. However, laws passed by the Scottish Parliament apply to Scotland only.

Public law

Public law relates to the state in some way, for example detailing the method of government. The most important type of public law is 'criminal law'.

Private law

Private law, or 'civil law', states what your duties and rights are in your dealings with other people.

In pairs

Use the Internet to find out about Sharia law. Some Muslims would like to see some aspects of Sharia law incorporated into UK law. Explain why you are for or against this idea.

Making the law

The law of England and Wales is a system that has developed over hundreds of years from various sources and is still developing today. The two main sources of law are common law and statute law.

▶ The image of a female holding a sword in one hand and scales in the other is a universally recognised symbol of justice – an image that goes back to antiquity.

Statute law

Laws passed by Parliament are called Acts of Parliament, or statutes. They are proposed by the government as Bills, and have to pass through several stages in both Houses of Parliament (see page 30) before they become law.

Common law

Common law is an unwritten law based on the decisions of judges, and is not defined by an Act of Parliament. When a judge makes a decision, it is based on the past decisions (precedents) of judges in similar cases. If a point of law has not already been decided, the judge will set a new precedent for the future.

By-laws

Sometimes Parliament authorises laws to be made by another person or body. Local by-laws, for example, are passed by local authorities.

EU laws

As Britain is a member of the European Union (EU), all EU treaties automatically become part of English law. Also, the European Parliament can pass new laws as either regulations or directives. Regulations become law automatically in member states; directives tell these states to pass their own laws to bring the directive into effect within a given time frame.

European law has supremacy over the laws of any member country.

In pairs

1 Discuss what you have learned about the different ways in which laws are made.

2 Should judges make the law in common law cases? What are the advantages and disadvantages of this kind of law?

3 Parliament is now the main law-making body in the UK. Why do you think this is?

In groups

Discuss why you think most people obey the law. Is it because they have strong religious or moral principles, or because they are afraid of being caught and punished? Or is there some other reason?

For your file

Write a short article on 'Law' for an encyclopedia aimed at teenagers. You will need to explain clearly what law is and why it exists, and list two or three different types of law.

Civil law and criminal law

Aim To explore the two main branches of national law, as well as the court system and the different professions involved in the law (Citizenship 1.1b, 2.1a, 3b, 3c)

	Civil law (private law)	Criminal law (public law)
Definition	Civil law states what your rights and duties are in your dealings with other people.	Criminal law deals with behaviour that everyone would agree is wrong. These actions are regarded as offences against the State, even though people are often the victims.
Examples	Disputes over contracts, property rights, discrimination, trespass, marriage, divorce.	Murder, violence, misuse of drugs, driving offences, fraud.
Purpose	To defend the rights of individuals and settle matters between them.	To protect society and the citizens of the state, and maintain law and order.
In court	The claimant takes action against (or sues) the defendant in a County Court. A judge decides whether the defendant is liable or not. If liable, the defendant usually has to pay damages to the claimant, or has an injunction taken out against them.	The defendant is prosecuted by the Crown. Most criminal cases are heard in a Magistrates' Court. Defendants are found guilty or not guilty; if guilty they are punished by fines, a community sentence or imprisonment.

The court system

The diagram shows the system of courts in the UK and where criminal and civil cases are heard.

Civil courts

Criminal courts

County Court
- Hears most civil cases
- Presided over by a judge

Magistrates' Court
- Hears most criminal cases
- Presided over by a magistrate

High Court
- Presided over by High Court judge
- Hears important and complex civil cases

Crown Court
- Presided over by a judge, though decision is made by a jury
- Hears serious criminal cases
- Hears appeals from the Magistrates' Courts

In pairs

Look at the diagram. Write down three differences between how criminal and civil cases are heard in the courts.

Write 10 questions about the law and test your partner with a quiz.

Court of Appeal
- Presided over by three judges at a time
- The Civil Division hears appeals from decisions in the lower civil courts
- The Criminal Division hears appeals from decisions in the lower criminal courts

House of Lords
- Five out of the 12 Law Lords hear each case
- Hears appeals on points of law of public importance

European Court of Justice
- The highest court of the EU, based in Luxembourg

Guitarist Peter Buck, from rock band REM, thanked the jury at Isleworth Crown Court after being cleared of going on a drunken rampage aboard a British Airways plane.

FAMILY doctor Patrick Vinall saw his career end in shame when a jury convicted him of two indecent assaults. The former GP was given two 18-month suspended sentences at Sheffield Crown Court.

People in the law

There are two kinds of lawyer in England and Wales – solicitors and barristers.

Solicitors

- Advise clients on a range of legal matters, such as drawing up a business contract, buying a house and making a will.
- Most work for a firm of solicitors, some of which specialise in particular areas of law.
- Since 2000, solicitors have been allowed to speak for their clients in the lower law courts.

Barristers

- Will be contacted by a solicitor on behalf of the client if the case is serious. Barristers specialise in presenting cases in court (called advocacy) and mainly work in the higher law courts. They also give advice and draft documents.
- Barristers are self-employed, but they work as a unit collectively known as 'the Bar'.

MOTHER of five, Sasha Clarke, celebrated after a High Court judge ordered Milton Mowbray Hospital to pay her £50,000 in damages. Mrs Clarke had sued the hospital for negligence after she had lost her unborn child in a bungled operation.

In pairs

Discuss each of the three cases above and answer the following questions.

- What caused the case to be brought to court?
- Which type of court dealt with it?
- Who was the defendant?
- Was it a civil or criminal case?
- Who decided the verdict, and what decision was made?

In groups

Choose one of these situations:

- **A famous person believes that a newspaper has falsely accused her of having an affair.**
- **The police charge a man with murdering his wife.**
- **A young man is caught breaking and entering a house.**

Invent some details for your case and prepare a presentation – either as role-play, a cartoon strip or a transcript of part of the court proceedings for your case. Explain what kind of case it is and what happened when it reached the courts.

Criminal responsibility

Aim To explore how crime relates to young people, focusing on antisocial behaviour (Citizenship 1.1b, 2.1a, 2.1b, 2.2a, 2.2b, 2.2c, 3b, 3c)

IN LAW, you have to be a certain age before you are regarded as fully responsible for your actions. This is called the 'age of criminal responsibility'. This means that in England and Wales, you cannot be charged with a criminal offence until you are 10 years old. When you are 10, the courts will assume that you knew what you were doing when you committed a crime.

The age of criminal responsibility is a controversial subject. Two different views are expressed on the right.

Role play

1 Discuss what you think the age of criminal responsibility should be. Think about these questions:

2 Do children understand the consequences of their actions?

3 Should children be dealt with by the care system or the criminal system?

4 Is a child able to participate in his or her own defence?

5 Should parents be responsible for their child's behaviour?

> **Children of 10 know the difference between right and wrong. They know you don't hurt small children. We have children as young as eight, or even six, terrorising people on estates such as the one I live on. I also think parents should be held responsible for their children's behaviour.**

Lyn Costello, of Mothers Against Murder and Aggression, who wants the age lowered to eight years old.

> **I think that at 14 years old, children are better able to understand the consequences of what they are doing. A child of 10 who has committed an offence is more appropriately dealt with in the care system than in the criminal justice system. The European Court says that a child must be able to participate in their own defence, and I think a child of 14 is able to do that, but a child of 10 is not.**

Carolyn Hamilton, Director of the Children's Legal Centre, who wants the age of criminal responsibility raised to 14.

ANTISOCIAL BEHAVIOUR

SOME SORTS OF BEHAVIOUR can damage how an area looks, and affect the lives of people who live there. Anti-social behaviour includes rowdy and nuisance behaviour, drunkenness, intimidating people, vandalism and graffiti. The police, local authorities and housing associations have recently been given new powers to tackle this problem and make neighbourhoods safer.

Acceptable behaviour contracts (ABCs)

If the police or a local authority have evidence that someone's behaviour is causing problems for the community, they can ask the person to sign an acceptable behaviour contract. This is a voluntary, written agreement, listing a number of things the person can no longer do, like spend time in certain areas with certain people.

Anti-social behaviour orders (ASBOs)

If someone has committed a number of anti-social offences, they may be issued with an anti-social behaviour order. ASBOs are court orders, lasting for at least two years, that can stop an offender going to a certain area or spending time with certain people.

If someone breaks the terms of their ASBO, they can be arrested and taken to court. If they are found guilty, they may get a fine or a community sentence, or spend time in custody.

Dispersal notices

Another way that anti-social behaviour is being tackled is by dispersal orders. A chief police officer can put restrictions on places where anti-social behaviour is particularly high.

Police can order people to leave a dispersal zone after a certain time, and exclude people from the area for up to 24 hours.

Source: adapted from 'Anti-social behaviour', www.direct.gov.uk

In pairs

Read the article on the left.

1 Which kinds of behaviour that are listed do you think are the most antisocial? Are there any others that you would add?

2 What measures are being taken to tackle antisocial behaviour? Do you think they will be successful? Suggest other measures that could be taken.

3 Many reasons have been suggested for the increase in anti-social behaviour – lack of jobs for young people, run-down neighbourhoods, fewer police officers and no real sanctions. What do you think the main reasons are?

Role play

1 You are members of a local committee deciding what to do in order to reduce antisocial behaviour locally. Which of these do you think would be most effective?

- Provide more clubs and facilities for young people.
- Use tougher sanctions for antisocial behaviour, e.g. more custodial sentences.
- Increase the number of police patrols.
- Close pubs that serve alcohol to under-age drinkers.
- Set up youth action groups to involve young people in schemes to improve the neighbourhood.

2 What other actions would you recommend?

The Youth Justice System

Aim To explore the youth justice system and what happens in youth courts (Citizenship 1.1b, 2.1a, 2.1b, 2.2a, 2.2b, 2.2c, 3b, 4a)

The youth justice system deals with young offenders up to the age of 17. It consists of youth offending teams who work to prevent young people re-offending, the police, youth courts and institutions where young people are held in custody.

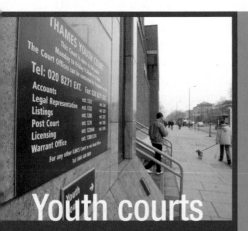

Youth courts

A youth court is a section of a magistrates' court which deals with almost all cases of young people under the age of 18.

Youth courts are less formal than magistrates' courts, They are also more open and engage more with the young person appearing in court and their family. Youth courts are essentially private places and the public are not allowed in. The victim(s) of the crime, however, may attend if they want to do so. Their needs and wishes will always be considered by the court and, through the youth offending team, they often have an opportunity to have an input into the sentencing process.

What is the role of a magistrate?

Magistrates are members of the local community. They are trained to:

- administer justice
- decide on questions of law, practice and procedure
- sentence young offenders in line with legislation and the Human Rights Act, alongside the welfare of the child.

Magistrates usually sit as a panel of three with one acting as chair who has the responsibility of addressing the court.

What is the role of the Crown Prosecution Service (CPS)?

The CPS presents the case against the young person. Its job is to present all the facts to the magistrates so that they can make a decision. It works closely with the police to gather all the available evidence to make the strongest case.

What is the role of a defence solicitor?

A defence solicitor represents the young person and acts in their best interests. The solicitor provides the client with legal advice on the charge, procedure and plea and speaks for them in court.

All young people appearing in court are entitled to be represented by a solicitor. The solicitor can be one chosen by the young person or the duty solicitor. Legal aid is available to pay for these services.

Source: adapted from the Youth Justice Board website

In pairs

1 In what ways is a youth court different from a magistrates' court for adults?

2 What are the arguments for and against allowing the victim(s) to attend youth courts?

3 Why is it important for a young offender to be represented in court by a solicitor?

For your file

Write an article for a teenage magazine with the title: 'Ten things you need to know about youth courts'.

Case Study: Trevor

Trevor (not his real name)* was arrested for stealing a Wii console, Playstation, DVDs and Playstation games. He was summoned to appear at the local youth court.

Trevor was accompanied to court by his father and, on the advice of his solicitor, pleaded guilty to burglary.

The prosecuting solicitor explained the facts of the case and how Trevor had sold on the goods to a market trader from whom they had been recovered by the police.

Trevor's solicitor then spoke on his behalf, stressing that although it was clear that Trevor had at times made some questionable decisions, the whole experience had had a devastating effect on him.

The magistrates took into account the comments made about Trevor and his situation by a member of the Youth Offending Team and decided to give him a supervision order for nine months.

*The press are allowed to reveal the names of young offenders only in exceptional cases.

Crown courts

In very serious cases, a young person charged with an offence will have to appear in a Crown Court to be tried before a judge and jury. These offences include murder, rape and robbery.

Juries – In England, juries consist of 12 adults chosen at random from the electoral register. The jury decides whether a defendant in a Crown Court is innocent or guilty. Juries are advised by the judge before they come to their verdict. Trial by jury is regarded as one of the strengths of the English justice system, although the government has suggested restricting jury trials in many cases.

In groups

Should the names of young offenders be made public whatever their offence and whatever their age? Give reasons for your view.

Role play

"Jury trials are an expensive waste, as juries often make the wrong decision."

"Trial by jury is a time-honoured way of ensuring that a person gets a fair trial."

"A judge has seen it all before – whereas a jury hasn't – and is far more likely to reach the right decision because a judge knows the law."

1 Discuss whether you believe that trial by jury should be restricted to only certain serious cases.

2 Role-play the case of a young person who has been caught stealing a car and has been arrested for the first time.

For your file

Write an article on the system of trial by jury for an encyclopedia for teenagers. Include a short history, an explanation of how the system works, and a summary of any controversial issues. Visit www.cjsonline.org for more information.

Punishment and sentencing

Aim To explore the kinds of sentencing available to the courts, focusing especially on the use of prisons (Citizenship 1.1a, 2.1a, 2.1b, 2.2a, 2.2b, 2.2c, 3b, 3c)

Sentencing

A sentence is a punishment imposed on someone who has been found guilty in a criminal court. Except in murder cases (when a life sentence is automatic) and a few other cases, the judge or magistrates can choose from a wide range of sentences.

The sentence always depends on all the circumstances of the particular case and of the person involved. In many cases the law states maximum or minimum sentences or fines, but within these limits there is a large measure of choice.

The main choices are:

■ **A custodial sentence**: Sending the offender to prison, a young offender institution, a secure training centre, or to an accommodation centre.

■ **Fining the offender**, ordering them to pay compensation to the victim, or both. The amount of the fine or compensation will depend on how wealthy the offender is.

■ **An order controlling the conduct or activity of the offender**, e.g. a drug rehabilitation programme, regular reporting to a probation officer or to the Youth Offending Team, undertaking some form of community punishment or unpaid community work, or going to an attendance centre.

■ **A parenting order**: The courts can make orders for those who are responsible for under-18s, to help the parent or guardian control the activities of the young person.

In pairs

1 Discuss and list the advantages and disadvantages of custodial and alternative sentences.

2 'The main purpose of a sentence should be to try to help the offender from committing further crimes.' Discuss this view. Which of the five reasons for choosing a sentence do you think is the most important?

The main reasons behind choosing the different types of sentence are:

■ **to protect others** – prison makes sure that the offender can't commit crimes against the general public

■ **to help the offender** – training and activities encourage them to 'go straight'

■ **to punish the offender** – some crimes may deserve a strong punishment

■ **to deter the offender and others** from doing the same thing again

■ **to give something back to society or to the victim** for what they have suffered.

BARRING THE WAY

Statistics and experience tell us that prisons aren't working, says Lucie Russell, Director of the Smart Justice Campaign

PRISON ISN'T WORKING. Around three-quarters of young offenders and half of all offenders commit another crime within two years of release, at a cost of around £11 billion to the taxpayer; and it costs £37,500 to keep one prisoner in jail for a year – that's a lot to pay for a failing public service.

It is true to say that offenders cannot commit crimes against the public while they are behind bars, but it is worth remembering that all but a handful of offenders are released into the community, and that the majority of them re-offend. Of course, prisons are necessary. We need them to keep us safe from violent and serious offenders. But they do not turn people into respectable, law-abiding citizens. Offenders – most of whom are imprisoned for non-violent crimes – emerge from jail hardened, alienated and ill-equipped for life outside. They are also armed with fresh criminal contacts and skills.

It's been proved that community-based programmes for non-violent offenders are more effective at cutting crime than prison, and are a fraction of the cost. Of every 100 people who serve a community sentence, 11 fewer are reconvicted within two years compared with those who are imprisoned. Community programmes deserve more money and resources so that they can be delivered consistently throughout the country. It makes sense to tackle non-serious crime in the community, while at the same time freeing up prison space for dangerous criminals.

Source: 'Barring the way to success', *Big Issue*

"Prison worked for me," says Lee, 22

"I never want to go back there again," says Lee, who was jailed for 18 months. "I got drunk and was involved in a brawl. It's really tough losing your freedom. I spent most of the day locked in a cell with a person I'd never have spoken to outside. People who say prison isn't a deterrent don't know what they're talking about. It's humiliating and degrading, but at least I got the opportunity to do some training, and I've now got myself a better job than I had before. But basically prison was hell. I'm determined I'll never, ever go there again."

In groups

Discuss whether you think prison is a bad way of punishing criminals. Or do you agree with Lee that prison works?

29

The UK Parliament

Aim To understand what the UK Parliament is and what it does (Citizenship 1.1a, 1.1d, 2.1a, 3c, 3d, 3e, 4a)

How the UK Government works

The Government in the UK is made up of three parts:

1 Executive – Responsible for making day-to-day decisions, such as how to spend money raised through taxation. The head of the executive is the Prime Minister.

2 Legislature – The section of Government that makes and amends laws (Parliament): the House of Commons, the House of Lords and the Monarchy (see right). The Prime Minister is head of the legislature.

3 Judiciary – Made up of judges who interpret laws that the legislature has passed. Individual cases are then brought before a judge who decides whether or not the law has been broken and, if necessary, what corrective steps a person needs to take.

The origins of Parliament lie in medieval times.

When the monarch needed to raise large amounts of money, nobles formed a Great Council (later the House of Lords). The Great Council also consisted of local people – commoners (later the House of Commons).

At this time, the monarch held absolute power. Over time, power has transferred from the monarch to the House of Commons. However, some power is held by the House of Lords.

The Cabinet and the Opposition

The Cabinet is the main executive committee of Government made up of between 20 and 25 ministers appointed by the Prime Minister. It makes key decisions and provides leadership to the Government. The three top members of the Cabinet are:

1 The Chancellor – finance
2 The Home Secretary – law and order
3 The Foreign Secretary – foreign policy with other countries.

Watching the work of the Cabinet closely is the Shadow Cabinet – the main figures of the second-largest political party in the House of Commons. The head is the Leader of the Opposition. The role of the Opposition and the Shadow Cabinet is to oppose the Government and offer alternative courses of action.

In groups

What is the difference between the Cabinet and the Shadow Cabinet? Draw up lists of key members of the Cabinet and Shadow Cabinet. Use the Internet to help you to compile the lists.

The House of Commons

There are 659 members of the House of Commons, including the leaders of all the main political parties. In 2005, these members included 128 women and 15 MPs from ethnic minorities. However, both groups are still significantly under-represented.

The House of Commons has 15 select committees, made up of 10–20 MPs, who look at one specific area of parliamentary business. For example, the work of the Home Secretary – who oversees the police, domestic security, and fighting crime – is scrutinised by the Home Affairs Select Committee.

The House of Lords

The House of Lords also scrutinises legislation, considers motions and holds debates. It has four select committees. The House of Lords usually agrees with the House of Commons. However, it frequently proposes amendments to legislation and sometimes it refuses to pass a bill. But it can reject a bill only three times within one year. After this the bill becomes law.

What the UK Parliament does

Parliament has several different functions:

- ■ To debate major, current issues of political importance.
- ■ To make laws. Most laws in the UK are made by Parliament. However, local councils can pass minor, local laws ('by-laws').
- ■ To scrutinise and debate laws that are passed in Europe. More and more decisions are made in Europe, with legal force across the European Union (EU) (see page 21).
- ■ To agree a budget, including the income and expenditure for the government each year, and to scrutinise how this money is spent.

Who is in the House of Lords?

In 2009 the House of Lords contained about 750 members, made up of different groups who have been appointed in the following ways:

Life peers – about 630 appointed by the government. Life peers include 12 senior judges, known as the Law Lords. These Law Lords also sit as the highest court in the UK. There are also 26 archbishops and bishops, appointed by the Church of England.

Elected hereditary peers – The House of Lords Act 1999 ended the right of about 700 hereditary peers to sit and vote in the House of Lords. Now there are only 92 hereditary peers who are elected by various groups within the House of Lords.

Once someone is a member of the House of Lords, they cannot be removed. Some support this idea – political parties have less power over them as they cannot be threatened with removal from office if they don't support a particular party. Opponents say that the system of appointment of life peers allows the Government to fill the House of Lords with its own supporters. They argue that the House of Lords should be an elected body.

In groups

1 Discuss your views on life peers. Is the system whereby the government chooses who should be in the House of Lords the best way of selecting its members?

2 Research the different proposals for further reform of the House of Lords, then hold a debate on the motion 'This house believes that the House of Lords should be replaced by an elected House of Representatives'.

In groups

Look at the different functions of Parliament. Which do you think are the most important? Give reasons for your views.

Voting and elections

Aim To understand how Parliament is elected, to explore different systems of election, and to discuss what can be done to improve voter turnout (Citizenship 1.1a, 1.1d, 2.1a, 3c, 3d, 3e, 4a)

You and your vote – elections

Elections are held to choose people to represent us – in the House of Commons, the European Parliament, in regional assemblies, and on local councils. You have to be 18 or over in order to vote.

First past the post

The country is divided into 646 areas, known as constituencies. One member of Parliament (MP) is elected in each constituency.

The present system of voting is known as 'first past the post'. It produces clear election results – the candidate with the most votes wins.

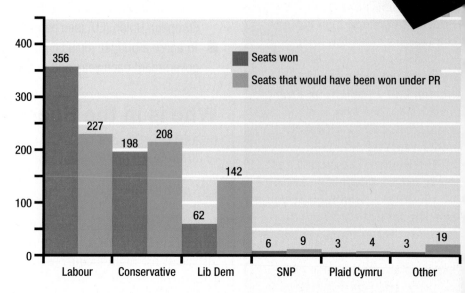

▲ Graph showing showing seats won in Great Britain in the 2005 General Election, and seats that would have been won if PR had been used (Source: Electoral Reform Society)

Proportional representation

However, the 'first past the post' system does allow a candidate to be elected on a minority of votes. For instance, one candidate may get 40% of the votes, another 35%, and another 25%. Over 60% of the voters have not supported the winning candidate – but they have not been allowed to register a preference for more than one candidate.

The alternative is proportional representation (PR) where candidates *can* register a preference for more than one candidate and the result is that the number of votes a party receives reflects closely the final number of seats that the party gains in the House of Commons.

Critics of PR argue that it does not allow close links between a single MP and a small constituency as, instead, a group of MPs would represent a larger area. Also, PR does not produce decisive results with one party with an overall majority.

In groups

1 Discuss which system of election you prefer and why.

2 Should there be a system of PR to ensure all parties are fairly represented? Or is it more important for each local area to have one dedicated MP?

> "I like 'first past the post'. It's simple. You put a cross by the candidate you support, and the one with the most votes wins." Tariq, Birmingham

> "PR is more democratic – minor parties don't lose out." Mel, Coventry

> "First past the post works – one party usually gets a clear majority. And that means things actually get done." Gywneth, North Wales

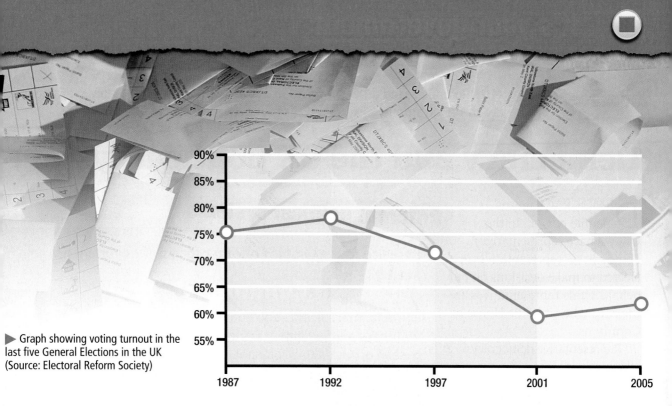

▶ Graph showing voting turnout in the last five General Elections in the UK (Source: Electoral Reform Society)

Is it worth voting?

Some people don't vote because they forget, or to make a political statement. Many people simply do not care, or feel that their vote does not make a difference. This is known as 'voter apathy'.

Get Out the Vote

Because of the low turnouts in elections, all the main political parties have been supporting 'Get Out the Vote'. The idea has been to get more people, especially young people, voting and involved in politics.

> "I used to vote, but I gave up at the 2001 General Election. The main parties are just the same, so what's the point?" **Michael, Kent**

> "I always vote. People died to protect right to vote. I respect that." **Glenda, Manchester**

> "I vote in the General Election because it's important, but I don't usually vote in local council elections – I don't know what's going on." **Angus, Glasgow**

> "Because of the electoral system, I don't vote. It doesn't matter – I've had the same MP for the last 20 years." **Toni, Newcastle**

▪▪ In groups

'Get Out the Vote' suggestions for ways of encouraging people to vote include: opening polling stations in supermarkets, holding elections on Sundays, and allowing Internet voting.

Discuss these suggestions. Which do you think would be most effective? Research these ideas on the Internet and write a statement saying which ones you would introduce and why.

▪▪ In groups

1 Is voter apathy a serious problem? Why do you think it is on the increase?

2 What do you learn from the statements above about why people vote or choose not to vote?

3 Would you vote in a General Election, a local council or European election? Give reasons for your views.

▪▪ In groups

Hold a debate on the motion: 'This house believes that it should be compulsory for adults to vote in UK general elections'.

Aim To understand different forms of government and what the key characteristics are of the UK's political system (Citizenship 1.1a, 1.1d, 2.1a, 3c, 3d, 3e, 4a)

Democracy and the UK political system

DEMOCRACY means 'people power'. In the UK, we have representative democracy – representatives are elected to make decisions on our behalf. These representatives are the MPs who sit in the House of Commons .

Representative democracy allows the opinions of a large number of people to be heard. It also allows speedy decision-making – it would be impossible for all 60 million people in the UK to be involved in every decision that is made.

However, representative democracy can create a distance between ordinary people and the politicians they elect to work on their behalf. In addition, very few independent politicians are elected. Instead, politicians form parties to achieve their aims and objectives.

Politicians try to keep in touch with the people they represent in a number of ways. Political parties organise focus groups to find out people's opinions and concerns and communicate with the public through the press, TV and Internet.

Individual MPs meet their constituents by attending local events and running surgeries where people can go to discuss issues and problems. They also distribute regular newsletters throughout their constituencies.

Different political systems

Here are four examples of other forms of government.

China – a Communist state

In China, there is only one political party, the Communist party. All others are forbidden. Views are sought at a local level, then passed upwards to a regional level, and finally to a national level. Supporters of this system call it 'grassroots democracy' as decisions flow upwards from a local area to the centre. Critics say this prevents freedom of speech and that it is open to corruption.

▼ Tens of thousands of students march towards Tiananmen Square in Beijing, 4th May 1989

Switzerland – direct democracy

In Switzerland, the government is a loose collection of areas called cantons (devolved government). Many decisions are made by the local population via referenda. This is known as direct democracy, allowing people a direct say. The system can be expensive, as holding referenda costs money and different decisions can be produced in different parts of the country.

Iran – a theocracy

A theocracy is where the Government is based on a particular religious group. In Iran, it is a Muslim state. A Muslim leader, called the Ayatollah, holds absolute power.

Iran still has a parliament and a President, both of which are elected. However, they can be overruled by the Ayatollah, who holds absolute power.

In 2009, Iran held a presidential election. The result was challenged by the main opposition candidate. The Government responded by cracking down on opposition protests, including intimidating and arresting the opposition, and putting some key figures on trial for treason.

▲ Robert Mugabe at the official opening of parliament of Zimbabwe in Harare, October 2009

Zimbabwe – a dictatorship

A dictatorship is when one person holds absolute power – in Zimbabwe in 2009 this is President Robert Mugabe. He holds this position through illegal means: by fixing the democratic elections and by intimidating and arresting the opposition. This form of government is undemocratic and can be violent.

In groups

Discuss the similarities and differences between each of the four systems of government. Talk about how living in these countries would be different compared to life in a representative democracy such as the UK.

In groups

"The scandal over MPs' expenses showed just how much MPs have lost touch with the general public."

"MPs do their best to communicate with the people they represent."

Discuss these views. How effective are such things as focus groups in helping people to be involved in policy-making? Suggest other ways that the public can be consulted about political decisions. For example, should there be more referenda on key issues?

For your file

"For all its flaws, a representative democracy is the best system of government." Say why you agree or disagree with this view.

Local government

Aim To understand what local government is and how it functions (Citizenship 1.1a, 2.1a, 3d, 4a, 4b)

What is local government?

Local government deals with local issues. Every area in the UK has some sort of local council, made up of elected members called councillors.

The idea of local government is to elect people who have good local knowledge to make informed decisions about local issues. For example, it is better for a group of local councillors to make a decision about building a new road nearby than for a civil servant in London to make the decision.

Different types of local government

Local government has either one or two main levels: in Scotland, Wales, Northern Ireland, London, or in major cities, there is probably one local council responsible for all local services. These are called Unitary Authorities in towns, and Metropolitan Boroughs in cities.

In the remaining areas of England, excluding most major cities, there are two main levels of local government: County Councils and District Councils. County Councils are responsible for education, social services and local transport. Within these, there are several smaller District Councils. These are responsible for planning, rubbish collection, housing and leisure facilities.

Local councillors
– who are they and what do they do?

Local councillors are ordinary members of the public who are elected to represent a local area – or ward. Wards can elect up to three councillors, depending on what type of council they represent and how large it is.

Local councillors have a number of duties:

■ attending council meetings every four to six weeks to debate issues and make decisions.

■ representing the council at meetings of the local authorities responsible for public services e.g. the fire or police service.

■ trying to solve the problems of local people.

In pairs

Find out who your local councillors are by visiting your local council's website. Which political parties do they belong to, and what areas of responsibility do they have?

In pairs

Think about your local area. What problems could your local councillor help to sort out? For example, what could be done to make your community stronger and safer? How could more opportunities be provided for young people? Draft an e-mail asking your councillor for help with a local problem.

STANDING TO BE
a local councillor

In order to stand as a local councillor, you have to:

- be over 18 years of age
- have a connection to the area.

You cannot become a councillor if you have been made bankrupt in the last five years, as you will be making decisions about public money!

Local councillors receive an allowance to compensate for the time they must take off work. They can also claim expenses for travelling to meetings. Councillors are also entitled by law to take time off work in order to fulfil their duties.

In order to encourage applications from a variety of people, the Government has suggested reducing the number of councillors, but offering the remaining councillors a full-time salary for a full-time job.

▲ Nathan Khan, the UK's youngest councillor, elected in September 2009, aged 18 – pictured with Chris Huhne MP.

Case study: Planning decisions

One of the powers councils have is the power to make planning decisions. If anyone wants to build a new road, extend their house, change a shop into several small flats, or make any other major change to their property, they must first get the permission of the council's planning department.

If the planning application conforms with the local plan, the application will be accepted. If it is rejected, the person making the application can appeal to the government.

Planning applications

Sometimes, the local council will demand money from a developer, in return for allowing a planning application.

Imagine that a developer wants to build 100 new flats in your local area. Role-play a meeting in which a group of councillors discusses what it will demand in return for planning permission. Think of examples of what the councillors might demand, such as a new playground for children who will move into the flats; a new road so the flats can be easily accessed; landscaping to hide the flats from view of the local residents; or a new community centre. Give reasons for your ideas.

In groups

1 Should local councillors be full-time? Or is it better to have part-time councillors who can bring experience from other areas? Give reasons for your views.

2 The age at which you can become a councillor was recently reduced from 21 to 18. What are the arguments for and against reducing it to 16?

In pairs

1 Are there any planning decisions you would like to see made in your local area?

2 Are there any past decisions (for example, the building of a controversial road or flats) that you disagree with? Give reasons for your views.

Aim To examine how local government could be reformed in order to reduce the democratic deficit that exists in UK politics (Citizenship 1.1a, 2.1a, 3d, 4a, 4b)

What is the democratic deficit?

One of the key functions of a democracy is to involve the people. However, in local government the number of people voting has fallen to 25%. This has created a gap between the government and people who do not vote – the democratic deficit. Some people feel that local government does not solve the problems they are interested in. As a result they become indifferent to politics, leading to voter apathy. One idea is to change the voting system (see page 33).

Changes within local government

Directly elected mayors

In 2002, local councils were given the power to hold referenda so that people could decide whether to directly elect a mayor. The mayor would then be responsible for all decisions, scrutinised by local councillors.

People living in some areas have voted in favour of directly elected mayors. Supporters argue that this leads to quick decision-making for which one individual is responsible. Critics of the system argue that it gives one person too much power. People in other areas have voted against having a directly elected mayor.

▲ The Mayor of London, Boris Johnston, who is the chief decision-maker in the devolved London Government.

▶ Stuart Drummond became the first directly elected Mayor of Hartlepool in 2003, when he won as a joke candidate, posing as the town's football mascot. In 2007, he was re-elected, as a more serious candidate in a grey suit.

🔘 In groups

Discuss the following views, and say why you agree or disagree with them.

"I like the idea of directly elected mayors. Having one person responsible for local government in each council is a good idea." Douglas, Watford

"We elect councillors, so they should all be involved in as much decision-making as possible." Katherine, Oxford

"Local councils don't make a difference – it's the Houses of Parliament that really matter." Tony, Plymouth

Involving local people

▪ Residents' associations

In some areas, such as parts of Birmingham and London, local residents would like more influence over decisions. They have set up local residents' associations to voice their views.

▪ Local referenda

Another possibility is to hold local referenda where, on controversial decisions, there could be a vote held by all the residents.

▪ Neighbourhood management

Neighbourhood management is part of the local council, with the power to make decisions and control small budgets. Each area would hold regular elections to elect an Executive Committee.

Neighbourhood management also includes local people who represent the views of residents in one particular street. They report any problems in the area to the local council.

❖❖ In groups

Look at the three different ways of involving local people in local decisions (above). Which do you think works best? Give reasons for your views.

Involving young people

Pressure groups, such as the British Youth Council, say there is a particular democratic deficit among young people, Election turnout is lower for people aged under 25, and only people aged over 18 can vote.

One solution has been to set up a Youth Parliament. Young people, aged 14–18, gather together to discuss local politics. They then elect one person to be the member of the Youth Parliament for their local area.

Another idea has been to create a local Youth Council – young people who meet to discuss local problems.

Case study: A congestion charge for Manchester?

In December 2008, a referendum was held in the Manchester area on whether to introduce a congestion charge. This would have meant a cost of £5 per day to drive through Manchester City Centre.

More than one million people voted in the referendum. The scheme was rejected by 79% of voters amid a turnout of 53.2% across ten metropolitan boroughs.

Supporters of the referendum say it was necessary in order for local people to have their say on such an important issue. Critics argue that the referendum was a waste of money, with 46.8% of people not bothering to vote, and the plan being rejected by a large majority of those who did.

◀ Members of the UK Youth Parliament being addressed by the Speaker of the House of Commons.

❖❖ In groups

How could more young people be involved in local decision-making in your area? Make a list of action points, then compare your ideas with those of other groups.

Local government

What is devolution?

Devolution means the transfer of power from one central point to many smaller, different areas. At a national level, this means the UK Parliament transferring power from Westminster to the Scottish Parliament, or to the London, Welsh or Northern Ireland Assembly. At a local level, this means councils transferring some of their powers to local areas within the council, for example, through neighbourhood management schemes.

Devolution was introduced in Northern Ireland in 1998, in Scotland and Wales in 1999, and in London in 2000.

Case Study: The Scottish Parliament

▲ Holyrood – the new Parliament building proved very expensive to construct.

The Scottish Parliament held its first elections in 1999, using a form of proportional representation. There are 129 Members of the Scottish Parliament (MSPs). The Scottish Parliament has the power to make new laws, and to raise or lower taxes slightly from the level set by Westminster. Areas of responsibility include health, education, transport, the environment, social services and housing.

For the majority of major decisions, the Scottish Parliament has worked well. Major decisions include abolishing the student loan system in Scotland, banning hunting, and introducing free care for the elderly in nursing homes. However, in at least one area there have been problems. In order to house the Scottish Parliament, a new building was designed at Holyrood. The costs of constructing this new building soared – expenditure that was meant to be controlled by the Scottish Parliament.

In August 2009, the Scottish Justice secretary was asked to free a Libyan terrorist who had carried out the Lockerbie bombing, in which 260 people died. The request was made on compassionate grounds, because the terrorist was dying of a terminal illness. However, he was given a hero's welcome in Libya, causing international outrage. Critics of devolution say that the UK Government should have intervened and overruled the Scottish Parliament. Supporters of devolution say it was a matter for Scotland to decide, as Scotland has its own legal system, overseen by the Parliament.

Case study: The Welsh Assembly

▲ The National Assembly building – the Senedd – in Cardiff, Wales

The Welsh Assembly was created in 1999, following a successful referendum for devolution in 1998. Unlike the Scottish people, the Welsh did not vote in favour of tax-raising powers for Wales. This means that Wales has an assembly – it cannot pass new primary laws or raise taxes, unlike Scotland, which has a Parliament.

To date, the Welsh Assembly has worked quite well. While it hasn't dealt with as wide a range of issues as the Scottish Parliament, there are now some noticeable differences between England and Wales. The biggest of these is free prescriptions, passed by the Welsh Assembly in 2007.

Since devolution was introduced in Wales, there have been several coalitions, all involving the Labour Party as the dominant partner. After the 2007 assembly elections, Labour formed a grand coalition with Plaid Cymru. The current First Minister of Wales is Rhodri Morgan.

Does devolution really matter?

Opponents naturally say that devolution doesn't work, and point to low turnouts at elections for devolved governments. Supporters say that it does work, as it is another opportunity for decisions to be taken that reflect the views of a particular area. Perhaps more important is what actual practical decisions are made that affect people's day-to-day lives.

By contrast, the Scottish and Welsh National Parties believe that these countries should be independent, with their own Parliaments. Scotland and Wales would then be separate countries, independent of the UK, within the European Union. Thus, both parties are demanding referenda to decide whether they should become independent.

⚙ In groups

Discuss these views and say why you agree or disagree with them.

"Devolution is a waste of money – why can't all the decisions be made at Westminster. We don't need these extra institutions."
Jill, Norfolk

"Devolution is great, but it's just a stepping stone for full independence for Wales."
Gwyneth, Conwy

"I support devolution. But that's far enough, there shouldn't be an independent Scotland or Wales." Angus, Aberdeen

How can you change things?

Aim To discuss pressure groups and campaigning in your town or local area (Citizenship 1.1a, 2.3a, 2.3b, 3d, 3h, 4a, 4e)

What are pressure groups?

Political pressure involves trying to influence somebody to make a decision. For example, in your local area, a number of people may try to persuade a council not to build houses on an environmental site. These people may form an organisation to influence decision-makers. This is known as a pressure group.

Case study: Heathrow Airport

▲ Civil disobedience – breaking the law or making a point? A member of the pressure group Plane Stupid throws green soup over the business secretary, Lord Mandelson.

In early 2009, the Government announced the controversial expansion of Heathrow Airport by backing the plan for a third runway. This was widely criticised by pressure groups such as Friends of the Earth, Greenpeace, and Plane Stupid.

These different groups campaigned against the decision in different ways. Climate camps were organised, where protesters could discuss different tactics, attend training sessions, and in some cases, engage in direct action.

In the case of Greenpeace, a campaign has been launched to sell off small plots of land where the Government proposes to build the runway. This form of legal protest will force the Government to negotiate with many different people and organisations to get the runway built.

In the case of Plane Stupid, members have invaded airports to block runways and stop flights from landing – a form of civil disobedience. They threw green soup over the business secretary, Lord Mandelson, to highlight one issue.

In pairs

Do you think breaking the law to make a point can ever be justified? Give reasons for your views.

Research the arguments for and against a new runway being built at Heathrow airport, then role-play a TV interview in which a reporter asks a group of protesters to explain why they are opposed to its construction and whether they are prepared to be involved in civil disobedience as part of their protest.

Setting up a pressure group

If you decided to set up a pressure group in your area, there are several steps that you need to follow:

1 Choose the issue or area that you want to campaign for.

2 Check that there are no other pressure groups already concentrating on the issue you want to campaign on.

3 Decide on a specific aim for your pressure group, e.g. to stop the Bloggs housing development from being built on Nicetown's Green Belt; to provide facilities for young people in Smallville.

4 Choose a name for your pressure group. This should be something catchy, memorable and relevant to the aims of your group.

5 Decide who makes decisions that will affect your pressure group, and then target them. This could be the local council, your local MP or local companies.

6 Decide who you need to support your pressure group. This may include those people targeted in the previous box, along with members of the general public and the local media.

7 Decide how you will raise money for your pressure group.

8 Decide how you will try to gain public support.

9 Decide how you will get in contact with other groups that share your aims and ambitions.

10 Decide how you will measure the success of your pressure group.

Getting things done

In order to influence decision-makers, pressure groups use a variety of methods to persuade people to support their point of view and to get their message across, such as:

- writing press releases and letters to the press
- organising a stall at a local market or in a town square
- running a petition, asking people to support a particular issue
- holding public meetings
- asking people to donate money, or join their pressure group as a member
- organising publicity stunts, including marches and public protests.

 **In groups**

Imagine you are setting up a pressure group either in favour of or against the building of a new by-pass. Follow the steps in the flowchart, and then compare your ideas with other groups in your class.

In pairs

Which of the above methods do you think are the most effective? Why?

National pressure groups

Aim To discuss what pressure groups exist nationally and how they campaign (Citizenship 1.1a, 2.3a, 3d, 3g, 4a, 4b)

What pressure groups are there?

Issue pressure groups

There are many different types of pressure group. Some groups may only campaign on one particular issue. These are known as single-issue pressure groups. Examples include the Campaign Against the Arms Trade (CAAT), which campaigns to stop the manufacture and sale of weapons.

Other issue pressure groups campaign on a range of connected issues. These include groups such as Greenpeace, which campaigns about the environment, and Amnesty International, which campaigns on human rights issues.

The main feature of issue pressure groups is that they allow anyone to join.

Sectional pressure groups

There are also pressure groups that campaign on a wide range of interests. These are known as sectional pressure groups. For example:

- Business associations – represent the views of business and industry, such as the Confederation of British Industry (CBI).

- Trade Unions – aim to represent and improve the working conditions of their members. Examples include the National Union of Teachers (NUT).

- Student organizations, such as the National Union of Students (NUS).

◀ The Trades Union Congress (TUC) is made up of all the major Trade Unions in the UK.

The main feature of sectional pressure groups is that they only allow certain sections of society to join. For example, to become a member of a trade union, you have to work in that particular profession. To join the NUS, you have to be a student.

In groups

1 Which issues most concern you? If you were to join a pressure group, which one would you join and why? Give reasons for your views.

2 Imagine that a students' union is being set up at your school. What issues would you want it to campaign on? Draw up a list and put the issues in order of priority.

▶ Students protesting against university fees.

New social movements

A new type of pressure group, increasingly in evidence, is the new social movement. New social movements are different from the other two sorts of pressure group in several different ways. Firstly, they are much larger, involving tens of thousands of members. As a result, they often involve coalitions of pressure groups coming together to work on a series of shared objectives. Often, these coalitions will be informal, and change over time.

The example of the first new social movement occurred in the late 1980s in the UK, when a coalition of groups, including students, trade unions and socialist organisations, came together to campaign against the Poll Tax introduced by Margaret Thatcher.

Other more recent examples of new social movements include Jubilee 2000. This consisted of charities, church groups and trade unions campaigning against Less Economically Developed Countries debt.

Two new social movements are still very active in the UK today: the Stop the War coalition campaigns against military action in Iraq and Afghanistan, and the anti-globalisation movement campaigns against capitalism and the exploitation of workers in Less Economically Developed Countries by multi-national corporations and the World Trade Organisation.

Lobbying

Lobbying is a technique that pressure groups use to influence key decisions. It involves trying to persuade the decision-maker to accept a particular point of view. The word 'lobby' comes from the area known as the central lobby in the Houses of Parliament, where people come to meet their MPs to try to influence them.

In pairs

Some people think lobbyists are useful, as they help MPs to make informed decisions by providing them with extra information. Others think they put pressure on MPs and exert too much influence on their decisions. What do you think?

Youth Funds

Aim To understand what Youth Funds are and to draw up an application, including a budget (Citizenship 2.3a, 2.3b, 2.3c, 2.3d, 2.3e, 4a, 4b, 4c, 4d, 4e; Economic wellbeing and financial capability 4a)

Applying for Youth Funds to improve local facilities

What are Youth Funds?

When the government did a survey about local facilities for young people in 2005, teenagers agreed that they'd like to have a greater say in what projects were given the go-ahead. So the Youth Opportunity Fund and Youth Capital Funds, known as 'Youth Funds', have been introduced, giving teens the opportunity to give their local facilities a bit of a makeover.

There is £173 million in Youth Funds over the next three years, and it's all got to be spent by March 2011. Here are the best bits:

- you come up with the ideas
- young people like you decide who gets what
- your local authority has got to spend Youth Funds money on projects for teenagers in your area.

Who decides who gets the money?

Your local authority will have a Youth Funds co-ordinator. They will be able to tell you how decisions are made in your area. Some local authorities have set up panels of teenagers to help choose the best projects. Others are asking all young people in the area what they think the money should be spent on.

The Youth Panels and local authorities who hand out the Youth Fund money have a set of five best potential outcomes that they'll use to judge your project by. These optimum outcomes are set out by the government, who want to make sure that youth projects will really make a change in communities, especially those that have no facilities for teenagers to use in their spare time.

When you are making an application, you need to explain how your project will meet these outcomes. The outcomes are:

- improving physical and mental health and encouraging teenagers to have a healthy lifestyle
- providing activities and places that help young people to stay safe
- learning useful skills that will look good on a CV or application form
- giving teenagers the chance to make positive changes in their area
- helping young people fulfil their potential, no matter who they are.

Youth Funds in action

Youth Funds are helping teenagers across England with a whole range of projects.

South Gloucestershire – A project was funded to repair a narrowboat. Youth groups, including young people with disabilities, now use the boat and help maintain it.

Gillingham, Kent – Two girls who were trained in music and drama wanted to give free dance classes for other young people in the area. An award of £3,000 paid for the rental costs of a local hall and for the final part of a teaching qualification for one of the dance trainers.

Bath and North-east Somerset – A group called the Manic Skaterz have been funded to set up a skateboard park in an anti-social behaviour hotspot.

Kingston – An all-weather sports pitch was built, after young people who had been campaigning for the pitch for some time got together to present their proposal to the grant board.

North Huddersfield – Local young people received the funding they needed to set up an after-school computer club at the North Chestnut Centre.

:: In groups

Make a list of ideas for a project that you think would improve your local facilities. Share your ideas in a class discussion and vote to choose the idea you think will benefit the most people. Then draft a questionnaire and carry out a survey to see whether other people in your area agree with you.

Planning a budget for your project

You will need to attach a budget sheet to your application showing details of the cost of your project. Ask yourselves the questions below, then list the cost of each item your project requires and work out the total cost.

- Do not guess the cost of an item. If you are going to hire somebody to carry out repairs, for example as part of a project to renovate a youth club, get at least two quotes. If you are going to buy new equipment, research where you can get the best deal. But remember you want the most suitable equipment and this may not necessarily be the cheapest.
- Will you have to pay staff or hire a professional to run your project?
- Will you need to hire a venue for your project?
- Will the project involve transport costs?
- Will you have to buy any new equipment?
- Will you have to buy any materials?
- Will the costs be one-off payments or will you need to include maintenance costs?
- What other particular costs does your project involve?

oining a Youth Panel

Members of Youth Panels talk about their experiences:

"It gave me a confidence boost, because I know that I am making a difference and I am helping people."

"It's mainly about team-building and compromising. Having to work your way into situations, not putting your foot down. You've got to be able to compromise within the team."

"I hope it looks really good for my communication skills and I hope it looks really good for my CV as well."

:: In groups

Draft a detailed proposal for a project that would benefit teenagers in your area. In addition to a budget sheet, you will need to include an explanation of how you will evaluate the success of your project. Invite community leaders to listen to your proposals and to discuss them with you.

For your file

Write an e-mail to your local MP explaining your views about the Youth Funds scheme. Say whether or not you think the scheme should be extended beyond 2011.

:: In groups

Discuss what the three teenagers say about the benefits of being a member of a Youth Panel. Would you put yourself forward for election to a Youth Panel? Give your reasons.

A sense of identity

Aim To explore your sense of identity, and your feelings about image and becoming an adult (Personal wellbeing 1.1a, 1.1b, 1.2a, 1.2c, 2.1a)

WHAT KIND OF ADULT?

Adolescence is all about developing from child to adult. But, Janet Lake asks, what kind of adult do you want to be?

Becoming an adult is the main point of adolescence, so it's worth spending some time thinking about the kind of person you want to be. What qualities do you want to have? What skills and abilities? What characteristics do you definitely *not* want to have?

Draw up a table like the one below. (The qualities listed are only an example – everyone will feel differently about this…)

It may help to think about adults that you respect, especially those of the same sex, whether they are members of your family or public figures. And, of course, adults with qualities you don't admire.

QUALITIES I WOULD LIKE TO HAVE	QUALITIES I DON'T WANT TO HAVE
✓ Coping	✓ Indecisive
✓ Strong	✓ Nagging
✓ Dynamic	✓ Stressed

Remember, there is no right or wrong answer to the question "What kind of person do you want to be?" But the qualities you jot down will tell you a lot about your emerging identity.

In groups

1 Read the article on the right about designer clothes and the quote below. Do you agree with Wayne Hemingway that 'it's cooler to be an individual than look the same as everyone else'? Or do you agree with Damian that it's cool to wear the right brands?

2 Discuss your attitudes to clothes and why you dress the way you do.

"There is a lot of pressure on teenagers to appear cool. That means wearing the right brands. Like it or not, that's the way it is."
Damian

In pairs

1 On your own, draw up a list of qualities, as Janet Lake describes.

2 Share your list with your partner and explain why you have included these qualities in your list. How similar or different are your lists?

3 Discuss whether you think your lists will change in the next five to 10 years. If so, how?

4 What do you think your lists say about your 'emerging identity'?

SELF IMAGE

You look in the mirror and you are either pleased with what you see or not. You may be looking at your physical appearance – skin, hair, clothes, or the image you portray – being confident or shy. Our self-image plays an important part in how we feel about ourselves and how we think others perceive us. Our self-esteem, confidence and ability to communicate with others are closely linked with how we view ourselves.

Television, magazines and adverts tell us we live in a world full of beautiful people. The pressure to have the correct body shape, wear only branded clothes and be full of self-confidence is a tall order. Many young people compare themselves to these images and often come to the conclusion they are not meeting the standards set by the media. Thankfully most of us realise that these expectations are unrealistic. We realise that life is not like this, and how we feel about ourselves is much more important for self-esteem and confidence.

Source: www.youth2youth.co.uk

DESIGNER CLOTHES

Designer Wayne Hemingway lets us know what he thinks of that scourge of every parent – the 'must-have' designer clothes labels demanded by many of our kids:

Why r so many kids dressed in the identikit uniform of Nike/Adidas/Reebok et al? Parents argue that the kids demand it – well how weak-spirited and old fashioned of you! Explain to them that: 1. It's old-fashioned to wear logos; 2. It's cooler to be an individual than to look the same as everyone else, and individuals are the ones that go on and make money; 3. It's a waste of money! 4. It's daft to pay to be a walking billboard – shouldn't it be the other way round?

Source: www.fatherhoodinstitute.org

In groups

1 Discuss how important the way you look is to your self-image and self-esteem.

2 Do you agree that expectations set up by the media are unrealistic? Discuss what you can do to protect yourself from this negative influence.

For your file

Write a statement under the heading 'Who am I?' to describe your own identity. Think about the following aspects of your identity and write one paragraph on each:

- Your **personality** – the features of your character that make you the person you are
- Your **appearance**, including your clothes, and your attitude to your appearance
- Your **goals and ambitions** – what kind of person you want to be, and what you hope to achieve in the next 10 years.

Influences on behaviour and self-image

Aim To explore the influences on your behaviour and self-image (Personal wellbeing 1.1a, 1.1b, 1.2a, 1.2c, 2.1a)

Who influences your behaviour?

YOUNG, FEMALE AND BANKRUPT

Lure of a celebrity lifestyle leads to rise in women going bust

Young women desperate to copy the opulent lifestyles of footballers' wives and girlfriends are responsible for a surge in female bankruptcies.

Research shows that the majority of bankrupts under 24 are now women succumbing to the temptation for excessive spending sprees.

A survey found that women were 'far more likely' to spend irresponsibly than men as they try to emulate celebrities such as Victoria Beckham.

Many young women have become trapped in debt because they feel they need to keep up with their peers by buying designer clothes and displaying other 'trappings of success', the study said.

Source: Mail Online, 17 June 2009

PM Wants 'Diversity' to be Youth Role Models

'Britain's Got Talent' winners, Diversity, are teaming up with the Prime Minister to smash Britain's yob culture.

The group of 11 dancers from East London and Essex have so impressed Gordon Brown that he's taking their advice on future youth policy.

With their dedication to education and their motto "dream, believe, achieve" the PM reckons they are the perfect people to inspire today's teens.

Source: *Daily Star*, 15 August 2009

The importance of parents

When we are young children we believe our parents are God-like – 'all-powerful' beings who are in control of it all. We naturally trust them and believe everything they say, and this trust makes us feel secure.

Then, at some point, most of us have this illusion shattered and we realise that our parents aren't actually perfect. From that point on, we lose some of our childhood innocence and start to look at things – and adults – differently.

It can be a painful awakening.

But, although painful, this process can also empower us to be more in command of our lives. We can finally figure out who we are and make decisions for ourselves, rather than just echoing our parents' choices and identities.

Source: *Sisters Unlimited* by Jessica Howie

1 Read the two articles about celebrities and young people. What conclusions do you draw about how celebrities can influence the self-image of young people?

2 Tell each other about the role models you look up to. What qualities do they have that make them your role models?

3 Do you agree with Jessica Howie that parents lose their influence on you some time during your adolescence?

4 How important is it for your self-development that you break away from your parents' influence?

On your own, make a list of all the different influences on your behaviour, such as family, friends, role models, media, religion, teachers. Rank them in order and share your list with your partner.

KIND...	SULKY...	THOUGHTFUL...
MOODY...	CONSIDERATE...	SELFISH...

1 Discuss what you have found out about labelling. How can good labels be bad?

2 Think of some labels that you apply to yourself. Where have they come from? What are they really based on?

3 Challenge your labels and help your partner challenge theirs.

Give a teen a bad name: labels

Listen to what family members say about each other. Consider the nicknames, the stories told about each other and the jokes. These are the signs that family members are cast into roles and given labels to match.

> "Oh, he's the clever one in the family but he's got no common sense."
>
> "She's a bit of a tearaway."
>
> "My youngest is such a scaredy-cat, she's nervous about absolutely everything!"

Labelling is disabling

Although it may be true that your child is more fearful than other children, labelling him as 'fearful' may make things worse. Labels – good or bad – become a part of the child's self image. Although a label may start with a germ of truth in it, it quickly acquires its own force. A 'clumsy' child becomes apprehensive about picking up something delicate and, in a state of nervousness, drops it. More proof that he is clumsy!

Good labels, bad labels and labels in pairs

Parents often label their children by comparing and contrasting them. First children are often 'nervous and shy' and their younger siblings 'outgoing and sociable'. Some labels link the child to another member of the family – 'You're just like your father'.

Even good can be bad

Positive as well as negative labels have their downside. A child constantly labelled as the 'responsible one' in the family, feels he always has to be on his best behaviour. His 'real self' is both responsible and reckless. Sometimes he feels the desire to break out and be irresponsible, but the label inhibits him. He may also fear that his parents only like the responsible boy and if they see the 'real boy' they won't like it or him.

Source: www.raisingkids.co.uk

Challenge your labels

"If you have labels on yourself, like 'I am a slow learner', 'I am uncoordinated', 'I can't multiply', ask yourself, 'What's the proof?' Challenge your labels. When we give ourselves a second chance, and get some help, most often we can do it."
Andrew Matthews

Source: *Being a Happy Teenager* by Andrew Matthews (Seashell Publishers, Australia)

How do you manage how you feel?

Aim To explore how to manage difficult moods and emotions, focusing on anger and disappointment (Personal wellbeing 1.4a, 1.4c, 2.1b, 2.1d, 2.1e, 2.3a)

What is anger?

We all feel angry sometimes. Some people tend to become angry easily (have a 'short fuse'), and some have problems controlling their anger. Anger has consequences, such as hurting other people – more usually their feelings, but sometimes physically. The after-effects of anger often make a person feel guilty and ashamed, but anger is a normal emotion.

Anger generally results from our feeling helpless or unable to control certain situations. We feel as if we are trapped by circumstances and can't see any way out.

Expressing and controlling anger

The instinctive, natural way to express anger is to respond aggressively. Anger is a natural reaction to threats; it allows us to fight and to defend ourselves when we are attacked. We need a certain amount of anger to survive. On the other hand, we can't physically lash out at every person or object that annoys us.

Here are some ways to deal with angry feelings.

1 **Express your angry feelings assertively, not aggressively.** To do this, you have to learn how to make clear what your needs are – and how to get them met – without hurting others. Being assertive doesn't mean being pushy or demanding; it means being respectful of yourself and others.

2 **Suppress anger** and then redirect it. Hold in your anger, stop thinking about it and focus on something positive. Physical exercise is very effective, as is redirecting your feelings into a hobby or an interest.

3 **Calm down!** This means not just controlling how you act, but learning to relax.

4 **Find out** what is causing you to feel angry, and then find ways of dealing with that cause. Talk to others who are involved and try to find ways of removing the trigger.

5 **Avoid alcohol** – If you drink, you will have less control over your actions. Alcohol is most often the fuel behind violence.

ANGER FIRST AID

- ■ Walk away! Come back later.
- ■ Try to 'count to 10' slowly.
- ■ Take deep and slow breaths, concentrating as you breathe.
- ■ Go out for a run, walk or bike ride.
- ■ If all else fails, thump a cushion or kick a bean bag. (DON'T do anything that will hurt yourself or someone else.)
- ■ When you feel calmer, talk to those you were with at the time and explain why you were feeling that way – calmly!

In groups

1 Discuss what makes you angry and how you deal with your anger.

2 Which are the best tips in the article for dealing with anger?

3 When do you think you need to apply 'anger first aid'?

Source: www.cwgsy.net/community/mindinfo/anger.htm

Dealing with disappointments and failure

How do you deal with disappointments?

You apply for a part-time job and your friend gets hired. Maybe you get a new car and it gets stolen within a week. Or you fall in love with the guy next door and he falls in love with the girl across the street.

When these things happen, you have a few options. You can either:

- Ask yourself, **"Why do bad things always happen to me?"** This gets you stranded in self-pity – not a helpful option. While we feel sorry for ourselves, we never do anything to fix a problem.

- Tell yourself, **"It's not my fault."** This is another excuse to do nothing. Even if it's not your fault, the question is, **"What are you going to do about it?"**.

- Ask yourself, **"What do I learn from this?"** This is how you bounce back. You ask yourself, what do I learn, what else can I do, who can help me? Then you make a plan to deal with disappointment.

If you believe (or even pretend) that every event in your life has a purpose, you will learn from your disappointments. We are not here to be punished. We are here to be educated.

IN A NUTSHELL:
You are never beaten until you quit!

It's OK to be wrong

Let's say you try for the lead in the school play, and you discover you don't like acting. That's terrific. You've discovered something more about yourself. Tick it off the list. Now you can say, "Forget Hollywood!" How else would you know but by trying?

Imagine you begin a law degree and don't like it. That's OK. (I know – I started law and hated it!) How else could you know but by trying?

People become happy and prosperous by doing lots of things, making plenty of mistakes, and taking the time to learn from things that didn't work.

IN A NUTSHELL:
Failure is not an end; failure is a beginning. The question is: "Does failure make you bitter, or does it make you better?"

Source: *Being a Happy Teenager* by Andrew Matthews (Seashell Publishers, Australia)

In pairs

1 Read about dealing with disappointments and failure, and discuss whether you agree with the author's views and advice.

2 Think of a 'failure' or 'disappointment' that you have suffered and tell your partner how it affected you. Did it make you bitter, or did it make you better? How could you have dealt with it differently, and what effect might that have had?

Assertiveness

Aim To explore what assertiveness is, and how to be assertive (Personal wellbeing 1.4a, 1.4c, 2.1d, 2.1e, 2.2e, 2.3a, 2.3b)

How to be assertive without being aggressive
by Caro Handley

THINK OF SOMEONE who has a seemingly natural air of authority, who gets things done and is listened to without ever shouting, threatening, bribing, sulking or crying. There aren't many of them around, but assertive people stand out a mile when you come across them.

By contrast, there are plenty of aggressive people around who use bullying tactics and think they're being assertive. To be assertive is to be neither a doormat nor a bully. And what's more, it's possible for anyone to learn how to do it, with a bit of effort and patience.

Be clear and direct
Work out in advance what it is you want to say and then say it as clearly and directly as you can, with no extra frills. Sound as though you know what you want or what you think, and people will believe you and know where they stand with you.

Use few words
The fewer words you use, the bigger the impact. Powerful, effective people are always succinct. Try to listen more often than you speak.

Be positive
Make sure that you are friendly and warm without being slimy or toadying – smile when you ask someone to do something and always thank them afterwards.

Pay attention
People will take you far more seriously if you look directly at them and give the conversation your full attention. A hasty order barked over your shoulder or muttered while doing something else will make the other person feel as though they don't matter, and may also give the impression that you don't mean what you say.

Source: adapted from www.ivillage.co.uk/workcareer/survive/

For your file

Practise your assertiveness skills using one of the following situations:

- Your brother or sister has borrowed something without asking
- You lent your friend a CD and it comes back scratched
- Your parent lays into you for leaving the kitchen in a mess (it was really your sister).

Write about how you deal with the situation aggressively, and then how you deal with the same situation in an assertive way.

In pairs

1 Read the article on assertiveness, and discuss what you have learned.

2 What is the difference between assertiveness and aggression?

3 How assertive do you think you are, and how could you improve your assertiveness?

A quarrel a day...

... keeps the doctor away, says Anne Nicholls. An argument can be good for your health, as it is better to stand up for yourself than to bottle up your anger. But there are good and bad ways to argue. Here are some tips:

1 Bawling at your boyfriend

17-year-old Karen is queen when it comes to arguing with her boyfriend, Lewis. "It'll annoy me sometimes if he's been chatting to other girls or spending too much time glued to his PlayStation. He doesn't seem to notice I'm upset, so I'll have to pick a fight to let him know what's been bugging me."

FIGHT FACTOR:

Anne says: "During a row, avoid the 'And another thing...' trap. After all, if he keeps doing something you object to, why not just try to accept your differences and move on? However, if arguing does resolve things, it can only be positive."

2 Punch-up with parents

Rowing with our parents is far too easily done, but there is a risk of rowing with them almost out of habit. "I realised I was acting like a stroppy madam around my parents, particularly when it came to things like what time I'd be home at night," says Jade, 17. "The thing is, I know that, unlike a friend or boyfriend, I can say almost anything in an argument with my parents without worrying about losing them."

FIGHT FACTOR:

Anne advises: "Let your parents know that you value their love and care for you and they're more likely to consider your needs. Helping out at home, making them cups of tea, and chatting about their interests as well as yours shows them you are mature and will invite their trust."

Source: adapted from *19*

In groups

1 Discuss arguments. How exactly can arguing be good for your health?

2 Analyse the two case studies in 'A quarrel a day' and jot down factors that make the argument unsuccessful and unhealthy. What factors make it successful and healthy?

For your file

Write a piece for a teenage advice website entitled 'How to have a good argument'.

Aim To explore your changing relationships with friends and family, and how to deal with these changes (Personal wellbeing 1.1c, 1.4a, 1.4c, 2.1d, 2.1e, 2.3a, 2.3b, 3f, 3g)

How to get a better deal

DO YOU feel that your parents give you less freedom than you're entitled to – much less than your friends, for example? Usually this is because they genuinely worry about you, about how you'll keep up with your schoolwork if you stay out too late and too often; about their fear that you may be attacked if you travel home alone at night, or (if you're a girl) end up pregnant if you stay all night at a party; about their terror that you may have had an accident or be in trouble if you don't come home at a pre-arranged time. All these are to some extent realistic fears; they could happen. But these fears are relatively easy to deal with as long as they're brought into the open and talked about.

It's more difficult if your freedom is restricted just because your parents have fixed ideas about what 'ought' or 'ought not' to be allowed at a particular age, or if strict rules are laid down which don't seem to make real sense to you. It's quite reasonable to tell your parents that you're the only one of your friends not allowed to do something special – but it has to be done really tactfully. It's easy to rub parents up the wrong way by pointing out how much more freedom your friends are given by their parents. 'But Tom's parents always let him ...' is likely to be met with only one response: 'Well, your parents don't.'

Points to remember

- They see themselves as good parents. Bring home the friends who are allowed extra freedom, so that your parents can see that they're not wild tearaways who will lead you into deep trouble.

- Aim for small concessions at first. i.e. negotiate an extra hour or two out when there's no school the next day.

- Once you've won that concession, try hard to keep your side of whatever bargain was struck. If you do stick to the agreed limits, it's more likely they'll agree to your next request.

- Try to get them to say exactly what is worrying them, rather than merely saying, 'You're too young!' There's nothing you can do suddenly to age yourself, but you may be able to reassure them about specific worries.

Source: *Adolescence, the survival guide* by E Fenwick and T Smith

In pairs

1 Summarise what this article says about how to get a better deal.

2 Do you agree that understanding where your parents are coming from can help you get what you want?

3 Do you think putting this advice into effect will work? Or do you already take this advice?

Role play

Choose a common parent-teenager situation and role-play (a) how not to get what you want, and (b) how to get what you want, using one or two of these points of advice.

The trouble with friends

Speaking up

Let your closest friends know if you're upset by something they've said or done. It can be really difficult being honest with a close friend because you have to strike a balance between accusing them and getting your point heard. In any friendship it's important we tell each other when we're upset with one another. Anything we hold on to will only magnify itself and, however deep we think it's buried, it will inevitably rear its head later on.

If you do end up having a big row with a friend, then hopefully there will be a time when you decide to make up. It can be healthy to argue occasionally, because in a way you're saying that you know the friendship is strong enough to be able to have a fight and still be best mates at the end of it.

Letting go of friends

There are also so-called friends in our lives who aren't really good for us. Sometimes you have to accept that a friendship has changed and you no longer share the same interests. It's okay to know that you can move on from these friendships and create new ones.

The people you surround yourself with reflect how you feel about yourself. If you have respect for yourself you can begin to move away from certain people because you realise that you deserve better friends than them.

Source : *Sisters Unlimited* by Jessica Howie

In groups

1 Discuss what you have learned about friendships from this extract.

2 Have you ever been in any of the situations Jessica Howie describes? How did you deal with it? Could you have dealt with it differently?

In groups

1 "Men manage friends differently to women." Do you think this is true? List the differences between how a man and a woman would handle a difficult situation with a friend.

2 Discuss what you think Jessica Howie means when she says, 'The people you surround yourself with reflect how you feel about yourself'?

For your file

"My closest friend puts me down in front of boys" Samantha, 16.

Write a reply to Samantha.

Exploring love

Aim To explore what love is and how there are different kinds of love (Personal wellbeing 1.1c, 1.4a, 1.4c, 2.1d, 2.1e, 2.3a, 2.3b, 3f, 3g)

What is true love?

"Love means caring more about that person than you do about yourself."

Roshi

"Total trust and acceptance of someone."

Bill

"There is no such thing as true love. It's an invention of the media."

Fabian

"True love is a unique chemistry between two people."

Mary

"True love? It just means wanting to spend all your time with another person, have fun and share things."

Josh

In groups

1 Discuss the old idea of love that Misha had, and the new idea that she came to have.

2 What do you think true love consists of?

What love wasn't and what love is

Misha thinks about some of her early brushes with romance, and comes to see love in a completely new light...

I had the usual romanticised ideals of love. I could imagine nothing more fulfilling than being wanted and loved by a gorgeous boyfriend. I wished for the gaze of a boy – any boy – to fall on me. At first I went out with boys simply because I was so flattered to be asked.

I was thrilled the first time someone said they loved me, but then I would turn over in my head the various things that the words 'I love you' could really mean. I wanted to be told that I was smart and funny, and beautiful; sometimes I was lucky and got to hear just that, although later I wondered if the boy really meant it, or if he was simply using the right words to get him 'further'.

I relied on him far too much. In fact I doted on him so that I wouldn't be dropped; not because I was crazy about the boy but because I was dependent on the love he was supposed to represent. I thought that was love. All I was doing was setting myself up for self-pitying nights spent waiting for him to call, and missing my girlfriends and family as I gave all my spare time to one boy.

It took a long time for me to realise what was going on. That old saying that 'you are the only person who will never leave you' is so very true. We must learn to rely on ourselves, to trust ourselves, to respect and, most importantly, to love ourselves. It's one of the biggest lessons of our lives: to find true love, you must first love yourself.

For a long time, love had one definition for me: romance with a boy. Now I know that there are so many different kinds of love, and so many different motivations for loving. That the love of good friends and family are just as cool. That they might last a lot longer than the boy who's all over you today and bored with you tomorrow. Our need for love means that we seek it constantly and that we mistake possessiveness, lust, and giving up yourself for another, for love.

Source: *Girls' Talk* by Maria Pallotta-Chiarolli

Do you really want a girlfriend?

Peer pressure is not a good reason for starting a relationship with a member of the opposite sex. A boy who is going out with a girl just to impress his mates is not likely to make a very good boyfriend, because he's obviously going to be more concerned with what they think than what she feels.

It's nice to find the idea of female company attractive after years of boyishly denying their existence and trying to avoid them at all costs. But it is easy for boys to see having a girlfriend purely as a status symbol or image-booster.

Relationships that just bring grief are all too common and are ultimately pretty pointless. Where's the sense in having a relationship purely for the sake of it? In fact it is far more pleasurable and beneficial to remain single, and to spend time getting to know and developing your own personality and interests than rushing into a relationship.

Teenage magazines and teenage fiction on television are often to blame for urging their readers into believing that love affairs and relationships with the opposite sex are the be-all and end-all of teenage life. They aren't. You don't have to date anyone when you are a teenager, and you will still grow up to be a perfectly normal, happy and healthy adult. And in fact the more time you spend on your own, finding out about who you are and about your likes, dislikes, aims and goals, when you are a teenager, the more likely you are to sail comfortably on to adulthood.

Source: *Boys About Boys* by Nick Fisher

In groups

1 How important is peer pressure in the search for a partner? What can you do about this pressure? Do girls suffer from a similar peer pressure?

2 Do you agree that the media is also to blame for pushing teenagers into relationships they don't really want?

3 Nick Fisher says that the best reason for getting involved in a romance is a desire for a 'deeper quality of relationship'. Can you describe what would make a relationship deeper?

For your file

Think about these different types of love:

- romantic love
- possessive love (obsession)
- sexual love (lust)
- platonic love (love for friends and relatives).

Write a short play or design a cartoon strip or a poster to show these different types of love.

Separation and divorce

Aim To explore the effects of family breakdown on young people (Personal wellbeing 2.1d, 2.3e, 3i)

Dealing with family breakdown

Research shows that around half of all divorces will occur within the first 10 years of marriage – often when children are still living at home. In fact, one in four children will experience their parents' divorce before they reach 16. What effect does separation and divorce have on children and families, and how do young people cope with these difficulties?

In pairs

1 Discuss what you have learned about the effects of divorce.

2 Why did Jessica Howie behave in a self-destructive way when her parents were separating? How would you advise her to deal with it differently?

Surviving divorce

Divorce: It's a really hard thing to go through, says Jessica Howie...

I found my parents' divorce very painful and difficult. I was one of the last of my friends to have parents that split up and I thought I didn't have a right to be upset because everyone else had been through it before me.

Because I hid how I felt, I compensated by getting into drugs, booze and boys. When my parents separated, I reached a new level of self-destructiveness. I was 14 at the time and just starting to come into my sexuality and have boyfriends. What I really needed was a safe place to show my feelings, and to have more communication with my parents about how I felt.

If your parents have split, it's okay for you to be upset about it. It is a very painful thing to go through and you're having to adapt to a completely different family unit. We all have different needs at times like this and it's important to say them to our parents. Often they're going through so much themselves that they don't realise you're finding it hard as well, and they might even lean on you for support.

How you can help yourself:

- Tell your parents how you're feeling; if you have a sibling, maybe confide in them, too.
- Your friends will rally round if you let them know you need them.
- Speak up and even get outside help if you need to. Talk to your GP if you want. He or she may suggest counselling.
- If you feel angry, allow yourself those feelings. Don't try to protect your parents from your feelings – they are valid and important.
- Tell your parents that you don't want to feel as if you're in the middle of their arguments.

Even if everyone you know has been through their parents splitting up, it doesn't devalue your pain and hurt. It is a really hard thing to go through.

Source: *Sisters Unlimited* by Jessica Howie

Deciding your future

When your parents split up, usually your parents will decide who it's better for you to live with. Don't feel guilty if you have a preference, though – it's your life. But if you don't want to say, just tell them to sort it out between themselves. In this case, they may have to go to court and let a judge make the decision. A court welfare officer may visit to try and find out which parent you'd be better living with.

Then a decision has to be made about how often you see your other parent. Again, it's best if this is sorted out by your parents (with help from you) but, unfortunately, it doesn't always work out like that.

What happens if...

... one of your parents tries to stop the other one from seeing you?

The one who's being prevented from seeing you has to go to court and ask for a 'contact order'. This says when and where they are allowed to visit and for how long. If the court thinks one of your parents has got good reasons for not wanting you to see the other one, they will send a supervisor to be at the meetings.

... you don't want to see one of your parents?

Your other parent will have to go to court and persuade the judge that a 'contact order' shouldn't be given. This isn't easy because usually the courts think that it's better for children if they're in touch with both parents. A court welfare officer and a child psychologist may meet you to find your reasons for not wanting to see that parent.

Maintenance

Both your natural parents have a responsibility to make sure you're cared for and to help pay for the things you need. Usually the parent who isn't living with you full-time has to pay 'maintenance' to the other parent.

Source: *Tell It Like It Is: The Virgin Young Person's Survival Guide* by K. Masters

In groups

1 What decisions have to be made about what's best for the children when parents separate?

2 List five pieces of advice you would give to someone whose parents are splitting up, giving reasons for your choices.

For your file

"My parents have split up. I live with my mum, and that's fine but she's constantly telling me how terrible my dad is, which I hate. I'd like to see dad more, but I don't like to upset my mum. My dad has invited me to go to India with him. I'd love to do this, but how can I leave mum on her own?" Amy, 15

Write a reply to Amy.

Bereavement

Aim To explore the effects of bereavement and how to cope with them (Personal wellbeing 2.1d, 2.3e, 3i)

The effects of bereavement

IT DOESN'T MATTER what age you are when someone important in your life dies or leaves you. It is difficult to sort out your feelings and it doesn't help when people say you should be feeling a particular way. The simple fact is that whatever you feel is how you feel at that time. It may be difficult for others to understand you, but it does help if you can learn to recognise these feelings for yourself even if you cannot explain them to other people.

Probably the strongest feeling you will have is sadness. It is important to let this out – this is what grieving is. But you may also have feelings that are less obvious…

Numbness
Simply feeling nothing when you think you should be very upset is scary. Sometimes it's nature's way of letting us take things in slowly until we are ready to manage how we feel.

Worry
You may worry about the future and who will be there to look after you. You may feel weird if you find yourself talking to the person who has died or thinking that you can see them, but it's normal.

Anger
You may feel angry for no particular reason. It's hard not being able to blame someone when a person you love or rely on is no longer there for you, so some people blame those around them, such as the doctors and nurses, if the person who died was ill.

Guilt and regret
When someone dies, for whatever reason, it is very normal to feel that you could have done more or that you should have behaved differently. It's also natural to think 'If only I'd…'.

Whatever your feelings are when someone dies, they're natural for you at that time. It can help to talk to someone you like and trust.

Source: www.childbereavement.org.uk

Coping with grief

It is OK to:
- cry and feel low and depressed. You've lost a great deal
- feel angry, embarrassed and not want to talk about your feelings
- 'live in the past' for a while. It can help you to keep alive the memory of the person you have lost, but try not to let life pass you by
- have fun and enjoy life, forgive yourself for the fights and arguments and nasty things you might have said to the person who died
- go on living.

But it is not OK to:
- use drugs or alcohol to dull your senses. This can only act as an escape and hide the pain, not helping to heal it, and can lead to other problems
- do things with your anger that can hurt other people because you are hurting inside
- experiment casually with sex, just to get close to someone
- hide your feelings to protect other people still alive.

If you find yourself getting into this sort of behaviour, it is important that you seek extra help.

Source: www.childbereavement.org.uk

Feeling suicidal

We can be unprepared for the intense feelings that can follow a death and for the way in which a once familiar world is turned upside down. Faced with this devastation, some people find themselves thinking that the world without the person who has died is now too scary, lonely, or too strange to carry on. They might wish that they too were dead.

This is a common reaction, and for most people the feeling fades over time. If, though, you find yourself thinking more and more about killing yourself, then it is really important that you find some support and help to get you through this difficult time.

Source: www.rd4u.org.uk/personal/when/suicidal.html

WHO CAN YOU TALK TO?

- **Talk to someone you know, such as a friend, someone in your family, a teacher that you trust, or your doctor.**

- **Ring a confidential helpline such as ChildLine (0800 11 11), the Samaritans (08457 90 90 90) or Cruse Youth Helpline (0808 808 1677).**

IT HAPPENS TO US ALL

We still have hang-ups about death. Often we're just uncomfortable tackling extreme emotions. But, on top of that, death is closely linked to religion and faith, which we tend to think of as private. When we do discuss it, we bring out all sorts of euphemisms – it's hardly surprising if young children get confused. "Grandma's passed away." "When's she coming back?"

Ironically, children in the 21st century are surrounded by death. But it's only make-believe, a screen fiction – playground games, video games, action movies. "In poor countries, children have fewer problems with death," says Dr Colin Murray Parkes, a bereavement expert. "They see dead bodies, rotting corpses. Here people protect children from that kind of thing, assuming it must be traumatic. In fact, the opposite is true."

Source: The Issue: Bereavement, TES

In groups

1 Discuss whether you agree that children in different parts of the world have different attitudes to death.

2 Why do you think death is such a taboo subject in our culture? What effect does it have when people don't talk about it?

For your file

Write a reply to this email sent to a teenage online advice column.

"My lovely gran died suddenly of a heart attack three months ago. I feel so depressed I don't know what to do. I go round like a zombie most of the time, then I'm really snippy with my mum and my mates. I just feel like, why has she died and not me?" Sara, 13

In pairs

1 Discuss what you have learned about understanding your feelings when someone dies, and coping with grief.

2 List five things that you can do to help cope with bereavement.

3 List five things that you can do to help a friend who has just been bereaved.

On your own

Research how different religions or cultures deal with death. Talk to members of different faiths. How do their mourning rituals help them to deal with death?

Leaving home

Aim To explore the reasons why young people leave home, and what options are available to them (Personal wellbeing 1.2a, 1.3a, 2.2a)

Why go?

"Because family life is awful."

"To travel abroad."

"To go to college or university."

"Because my parents kicked me out."

"To live with my partner."

"To become more independent."

"To escape violence at home."

In groups

Discuss the reasons that young people may have for leaving home. Which are the three best reasons? Which are the three worst? Share your lists with other groups and justify your decisions.

In groups

Discuss what you have learned about how difficult life at home can be for some young people. How well do you think Lisa dealt with the situation? Would you have done anything differently?

Case study – Lisa's story

My name is Lisa. I am 19 years old. I'm not what you'd call a typical teenager who fought with their mum and dad all the time, but I had a very bad relationship with my mother. I was in and out of care from the age of 11. It was around my 16th birthday when she kicked me out. I felt like I was on my own in the big, bad world.

After a few weeks of sleeping rough, I finally decided to do something, so I went to the Social Work Department. They got me into a hostel and I finally had a bath, clean clothes and a sense of warmth. I started to spend a lot of time with people my age, and started to learn that I wasn't alone.

In 2002 my mother died. That was when I found out that all the time we were arguing, it was my mum being unwell. So now I no longer blame myself for what happened between the both of us.

I am now living in supported accommodation, I have had a steady partner for nearly three years, and I have enrolled at college. It's when you're hardest hit that you must not quit.

Source: www.leavinghome.info

Running away

When things go wrong at home, some people feel as if the only answer is to run away. Before you do this – talk to someone. Your parents are the best people to talk to because they can change things. Also, they may not be aware how you feel because you've been bottling it up. If you've got into trouble, they will have to know sooner or later, and will probably be more understanding than you think.

But if you can't talk to your parents, then talk to anyone you trust, such as a grandparent or a helpline worker. Running away may seem like an answer to your problems but usually it isn't. It's dangerous and difficult, and will almost certainly make those who love you sick with worry.

What three pieces of advice would you give to someone who is thinking about running away?

A place of your own

If you decide to move out, what kind of accommodation is available?

Private rented accommodation

Houses, flats, bedsits or rooms rented out by landlords are the most common types of housing available to you when you leave home. Often you will have to share with others, and the standard of accommodation may vary. Renting can be done quite quickly and easily. However, rents can be high, and most landlords ask for a deposit and one month's rent in advance. They also are often wary of renting to young people on benefits.

Social rented housing

This refers to flats and houses rented out by local councils and housing associations. You may have to wait before you even get onto a waiting list, and single young people come lower down the priority housing list than families and couples. However, social housing tenants have better rights and usually pay lower rents than people in private rented accommodation.

Hostels

Hostels (not hotels!) are special types of accommodation catering for young people. Emergency hostels provide rooms for just a few nights. Women's refuges are for women who have escaped from a violent situation at home. Hostels vary a lot in their size and standard, and often have waiting lists. They may, however, suit your specific needs for a short time.

Buying a home

Get real! Either you've landed the job of a lifetime or you've got very generous parents. Buying a property is not a serious option for most young people.

In groups

Discuss the advantages and disadvantages of each type of accommodation. Then design an information leaflet aimed at young people looking for their first place away from home.

Leaving home and the law

The law says that young people under 18 are in 'the custody and care' of their parents. This means that, strictly speaking, they need their parents' permission to leave home. In fact, if a 16- or 17-year-old leaves home without their parents' permission, courts only order them to return if they are in danger or cannot look after themselves.

Under the Children Act (1989), 16- and 17-year-olds who are 'in need' should have accommodation provided to them by local authorities. However:

- suitable accommodation for young people is not always available

- income support is not available to all 16- and 17-year-olds.

You cannot buy or rent a house if you are under 18.

For your file

Write a short article for a teenage magazine entitled 'Thinking of leaving home?'.

65

Aim To understand what prejudice is, to explore where prejudice comes from, and how prejudice can lead to discrimination (Citizenship 1.1c 1.2a b 2.1a 4a; Personal wellbeing 1.5a b 2.1a 2.3d 3a j)

What is prejudice?

Are you prejudiced? Most people think that they treat other people fairly. However, often we treat people according to opinions we have already formed about them. Here's an example:

Prejudice is when you have made up an opinion about somebody in advance. For example, assuming that people who shave their heads are more likely to start fights would be an example of prejudiced behaviour based simply on appearance. The truth is a lot more complicated.

We often fit people into groups – black, white, male, female, young or old, and when we put people into groups, we can expect members of that group to behave in a particular way. This can lead to prejudice. For example, you may know lots of young people who enjoy loud music and going to parties. It doesn't mean that all young people are loud troublemakers.

Case study: Robert

Robert was on his way home when he saw a scruffily-dressed teenager rush out of a shop clutching a purse. Robert got out his mobile phone to call the police and ran after the teenager so that he could tell the police where he was. He was surprised when he saw the boy stop and start talking to an old lady. Imagine his embarrassment when he found out that the boy lived in the same block of flats as the old lady, and that she'd been into the shop and left her purse on the counter, and that he was running after her to give it back.

In groups

Imagine these roles – mother, father, brother and sister. List the prejudices you think would annoy each person. Discuss what you think the most common prejudices are and why.

In groups

1 Why did Robert think the boy was a thief? Was it the circumstances or his appearance?

2 Have you ever misjudged a person because of their appearance or behaviour? Has anyone ever misjudged you?

3 Are some people more likely to be misjudged than others? Why?

Looking at prejudice

Part of a group or not?

We like to surround ourselves with people who are similar to ourselves because it is good to feel that you belong to a group. A group can be your family, people your age, your class at school, the members of a sports club or the members of a church. As humans, we immediately prefer those people in the same groups as ourselves; we have a natural tendency to be prejudiced against people who are different from us.

In pairs

1 List all the groups you are in. Write down ways you think these groups behave.

2 Compare your list with your partner's. Discuss whether these behaviours are fair. Or have you some prejudices about the groups you have listed?

In pairs

1 Look at the causes of prejudice below. Which do you think are the strongest factors in creating prejudice? Give reasons for your views.

2 List all the forms of discrimination that you think should be against the law.

3 What do you think are the most common kinds of discrimination in your local area? Give reasons for your views.

In groups

Design a poster against some form of discrimination. Compare your poster with other groups.

Where does prejudice come from?

There are many different arguments suggesting where prejudice comes from.

We are born with it
It's natural for humans to compete. In the past this was for land and food, now it's exams, sporting events, or for jobs.

It's passed on to the next generation
Think about the games you were encouraged to play as a child. Were boys encouraged to play football and girls to play with dolls? Such behaviour reinforces prejudice about the opposite sex.

Going with the majority
People find it easier to go along with what other people are doing and copy other people's prejudices.

Scapegoating
This is when it's convenient to blame a problem on one group of people, for example, blaming unemployment on illegal immigrants when really there are problems in the economy.

Narrow-minded or rigid views
Psychologically, some people have a greater likelihood of developing prejudices against new or unfamiliar groups, because they find it hard to accept new ideas and are more comfortable with familiar situations.

Prejudice and discrimination
Prejudice may be wrong, but it's not against the law. We all have occasional thoughts about groups which may be incorrect. However, if these thoughts become commonplace and we choose to act on them, this then becomes discrimination.

Some forms of discrimination are against the law in the UK. These include the following:

- Sexual discrimination
- Age discrimination
- Racial discrimination
- Religious discrimination

Fighting discrimination

Aim To understand that there are laws and equal opportunities policies to combat discrimination, and to explore what you can do about discrimination (Citizenship 1.1c, 1.2a, 1.2b, 4a Personal wellbeing 1.5a, 1.5b, 2.1a, 2.3d, 3a, 3j)

Discrimination and the law

There exists a wide range of laws outlawing many forms of discrimination, such as racial discrimination. There are several laws that the government uses against racist behaviour:

- **The Race Relations Act** (1976) and **Regulations** (2003) makes it illegal for anyone to discriminate on the grounds of race, colour, nationality, or ethnic and national origins.

- **The Crime and Disorder Act** (1998) requires racial crimes to carry a heavier sentence.

Equal opportunities policies

On a local level, many employers and local organisations have equal opportunity policies to make sure no discrimination occurs. It may include practical examples of what is not acceptable, such as sexual harassment and sexist jokes against members of the opposite sex.

In groups

"I think that discrimination against overweight people should be outlawed. It doesn't matter what I eat, I stay the same weight – yet people call me 'fatty'. I'm sick of being discriminated against." Martha

"I hate the way everything is designed for right-handed people. How about a law to prevent discrimination against the one in 10 of us who are left-handed?" Gemma

Do you think there should be laws to prevent discrimination against the people mentioned in the statements? Give reasons for your views.

Positive discrimination

Positive discrimination offers special opportunities for minority or disadvantaged groups. Supporters argue that this ensures that minority groups receive a fair access to things they would normally be excluded from. Critics of positive discrimination argue that it still produces discrimination, because it discriminates against those who would otherwise have access to those things.

"Positive discrimination is necessary so that minority groups can be fairly represented in education and government."

"All discrimination should be illegal."

In pairs

Look at these two statements. Which do you agree with? Give reasons for your views.

Taking a stand

The problem with discrimination is that many people don't know how to fight it when they encounter it. It takes courage. Here are six ideas for fighting discriminatory behaviour.

1 Don't ignore it, report it. If you witness discriminatory behaviour, report it to the police. Don't put yourself at risk of physical harm, but don't ignore the problem.

2 Complain – if you see discrimination on TV or hear it on the radio, contact the Advertising Standards Authority; if you read it in a newspaper or magazine, write to the editor of the publication; if you see it on a website, complain to the Internet provider.

3 Don't tolerate friends who express discriminatory attitudes or behave in a discriminatory way.

4 Don't vote for political parties, such as racist political parties, who openly discriminate against minority groups.

5 Don't buy CDs or DVDs made by musicians who express prejudiced views.

6 Don't accept arguments that people use to justify prejudiced behaviour. Find out the real facts for yourself.

Challenging myths about asylum seekers

MYTH: Most asylum seekers are just here looking for work.

REALITY: Most asylum seekers are not permitted to work.

MYTH: Asylum seekers take all the taxpayer's money in the UK.

REALITY: Not true. Asylum seekers do not get large handouts from the state and are denied access to many benefits others rely on. The UK gives asylum seekers less financial support than many other European countries.

MYTH: Britain is soft on asylum seekers.

REALITY: Not true. In recent years, the countries hosting most asylum seekers were Germany, Pakistan and Iran. Out of a list of 36 countries that took in asylum seekers in 2008, the UK was seventeenth.

MYTH: There is a higher rate of crime among asylum seekers.

REALITY: Not true. A recent report by the Association of Chief Police Officers confirmed that there is no evidence of a higher rate of crime among asylum seekers and refugees.

In groups

Look at the information about asylum seekers. Does any of it surprise you? Why? Do you think most people have an accurate image of asylum seekers?

Eating and body shape

Aim To explore attitudes to body shape, eating and dieting, and to explain what are healthy eating habits (Personal wellbeing 1.2a, 1.2b, 2.2a, 3b, 3d)

You and your body image
– be realistic

When you look in the mirror, what do you see? How would you describe yourself? How do you perceive your body? This perception is your body image, or what you think you see in the mirror.

Unfortunately a person's body image is often very different from their actual body. It is this distortion, this negative body image, that often pushes people to their limit to change what actually isn't there. Rather than fight with this phantom image, cultivate a realistic body image based on what your body can do, and how you feel, rather than how your body looks.

Many young people base their body image on what they see in the media. Young women want to be thin and willowy, and young men want bulging biceps and washboard abs. Yet what is shown on our TV and cinema screens and in our magazines and on websites are the exceptions rather than the rule.

In reality, base your body image on respect for who you are and what you look like as an individual. Don't compare yourself to supermodels or celebrities, or even to your friends who have naturally different body shapes.

Source: *Teen Issues*

What the celebs say

"I finally realised I don't have an A-plus perfect body – but I'm very happy and I'm not going to worry about a few extra pounds. Puppy fat is sexy." Drew Barrymore

"I couldn't care less about stupid diets. Eating is sensual and fun. I'm not going to let it be spoiled by calorie counting." Christina Aguilera

A false picture

What teens often neglect to consider is that even the celebrities themselves may not look in real life the way they do in their publicity photos. Computer touch-ups can slim tummies, give the illusion of muscle definition, remove flyaway hairs, and perfect skin tone, making a regular person seem flawless.

Source: *Kids Exercise*

 **In pairs**

Do you think teenagers are obsessed with their body images? Where do you think the pressure comes from?

DEVELOPING HEALTHY EATING HABITS

Top tips to healthy eating

1 Your body needs carbohydrates to give you energy. So fill up on rice, pasta, wholemeal bread, potatoes and cereals.

2 Eat five portions of fruit and vegetables each day. They contain vital vitamins.

3 Drink milk or eat other dairy products, such as cheese or yogurt, to give you the bone-building calcium your body needs.

4 Get plenty of protein. Meat, chicken, fish, eggs and beans all help to build and repair cells. Have two portions a day and snack on protein-rich nuts and seeds.

5 Cut down on fatty and sugary foods. Limit yourself to one serving or less per day.

6 Don't diet. Starving yourself of calories is definitely not a smart way to lose weight. Instead, eat regularly and exercise for an hour at least three times a week.

7 Drink at least six glasses of water a day. Water keeps you fit and active, while soft and sugary drinks actually steal water from the body to process the sugar.

In groups

"You can't be attractive unless you're very thin."

"Thin people are more popular."

"Exercise is a better way of controlling your weight than dieting."

"It's more important to eat properly than to try to lose weight."

"How you look matters more than what sort of person you are."

Discuss each statement, saying whether you agree or disagree with it, and why.

Eating disorders

A person who has an eating disorder has a problem with food and eating. There are three main eating disorders – anorexia nervosa, bulimia and compulsive overeating.

A person with anorexia is obsessed with their weight and their shape, so they deliberately lose weight by trying to avoid eating, or eating very little.

A person with bulimia is also very concerned about the size of their body. They go on binges, eating large amounts of food in a short time, then try to get rid of it by making themselves sick or by taking laxatives.

A compulsive overeater also eats a large quantity of food, but without getting rid of it. They eat for emotional reasons, rather than because they feel hungry.

Eating disorders appear to be all about food, but what triggers an eating disorder is a person's feelings about themselves and their situation.

In pairs

"I feel I'm overweight, so I'm thinking of going on a crash diet. My friend says it's the only thing that works. Is she right?" Marvina

Discuss this letter to a problem page in a teenage magazine, and draft a reply.

For your file

Design a leaflet for young people giving information about eating disorders. Useful websites to visit include www.b-eat.co.uk, the website of the Eating Disorders Association.

Aim To examine why many teenagers do not eat healthily, and to discuss how far junk foods are responsible for making people overweight (Personal wellbeing 1.2a, 1.2b, 2.2a, 3b, 3d)

Teenagers are getting less fit

Health experts say teenagers are less fit than they used to be. What has caused this drop in fitness? Most health experts believe there are two factors:

1 A change in eating habits. There's a greater reliance on fast foods, junk foods and ready meals, rather than on a healthy, balanced diet of three regular meals a day.

2 A decline in the amount of exercise taken. We travel more by car, bus or train rather than walking or cycling, and spend time watching TV or on the computer, rather than on outdoor activities that would use up excess fat.

In groups

1 Discuss whether you think the newspaper report is fair to teenagers. How accurate are the statements it makes? Do you know which foods are good for you? Are most teenagers unable to cook anything other than toast or ready meals? Are teenagers too lazy to eat properly?

2 Plan and carry out your own survey on teenagers' eating habits. Report your findings to the rest of the class and say whether they support the findings of the survey reported in the article.

Teenagers 'too idle' to bother with good food

TEENAGERS KNOW which foods are good for them, but cannot be bothered to eat healthily or learn to cook properly, according to a survey. Although three-quarters associate a good diet with long-term health, few can make more than toast, and most choose crisps and chocolate rather than fruit.

Among those who do eat fruit, laziness puts them off anything that requires peeling. "If we buy grapes, I eat loads and loads," a 17-year-old boy said. "Oranges you have to peel, and that's a chore."

Four out of ten teenagers surveyed did not eat breakfast. Almost half ate at a fast-food restaurant at least once a week, more out of idleness and a desire for convenience than for any other reason.

When they arrive at school, few teenagers eat healthily. Only one in six buys fruit, vegetables or yogurts. "In the morning I have cereal," a 17-year-old boy said. "But sometimes I can't be bothered so I just have a drink. At breaktime I might have three chocolate bars or a burger. Today I had a burger."

Diets worsen at weekends and during holidays. A 16-year-old girl was typical of the two in five teenagers who miss breakfast because they stay in bed. She said: " At weekends or in the holidays I don't usually eat until the evening because I sleep more during the day."

Few teenagers associate eating with regular mealtimes and most lack the skill to prepare anything more than a ready meal. While six out of ten knew how to use a microwave, fewer than a quarter had ever made a pasta sauce.

Source: *Daily Telegraph*

Crackdown on junk foods

THE GOVERNMENT'S top food adviser is considering harsh laws to ban junk food advertising and prevent firms from using celebrities to endorse products high in fat, sugar and salt.

The chairman of the Food Standards Agency warned that if the number of overweight young people was not reduced, life expectancy could start to fall.

In addition to possible bans on junk food advertising, other measures under consideration include:

- pressurising supermarkets to offer 'buy one, get one free' promotions only on healthy children's foods
- making shops replace sweets on sale at checkouts with healthier options
- labelling products that are

high in fat, sugar or salt clearly on the front of packets, possibly in the form of a government health warning
- banning vending machines from stocking sweets and crisps in schools and leisure centres
- putting a 'fat tax' on cakes, biscuits and processed food.

PUT VAT ON HIGH-FAT FOOD, URGES GP

Doctors are calling for a new 'fat tax' on cakes, biscuits and processed food to tackle the increase in the number of people who are overweight.

A British Medical Association conference is to debate if VAT should be added to all high-fat food.

Because most food is exempt from VAT, extending the tax would raise millions of pounds.

Dr Martin Breach, who is proposing the new tax, believes the money would cover the cost of treating the health problems caused by being overweight and might also change people's behaviour.

Source: *Daily Telegraph*

In groups

1 How far do you think junk foods are to blame for increases in the number of people who are overweight?

2 Discuss the proposed measures to try to reduce the amount of junk foods people eat. Which ones do you think would be effective?

For your file

"What does it matter what I eat and when I eat? There's too much fuss about healthy eating." Wayne, 16

Draft a reply to Wayne explaining to him why it matters to eat healthily and regularly.

When is the right time to have sex?

Aim To discuss what you need to consider when deciding whether or not to have sex with someone, to explore attitudes towards sex and how to resist unwanted pressure (Personal wellbeing 1.2a 1.3a, 1.3b, 1.3c, 2.2a, 2.2b, 2.2c, 3d, 3e)

Sex and you
– waiting until the time is right

The age of consent – the age when it is legal for a young person to have sex – is 16. Some young people have sex before they are 14. Some young people wait until they are older than 16. Many relationships build slowly: the couple become good friends, getting to become close mentally and then, perhaps, physically. Some young people are keen to explore the physical side sooner rather than later and the question of sex crops up – do you or don't you?

The most important thing to remember at this time is never be pressurised into anything you know you're not ready for, and that goes for all things, sexual or not!

Think about the following:

- Sex, once given, cannot be taken back.
- Moral aspects – some cultures and religions believe that remaining a virgin until after marriage is very important. Would you feel guilty or cause trouble if you disobey your beliefs?
- Giving the most intimate part of yourself to someone else should be a thought-out, loving and valued experience by both people involved. It should feel 'right' and without guilt.
- Everyone does not 'do it', despite what they might claim. If you want to wait until you are sure, that is your right and choice.

Sex needs to be discussed between the two members of a couple. Some couples want to take things slowly, especially if they're both young, or they plan to save a full sexual relationship until after marriage. Many religions still maintain that sex is only morally right when you're in a marriage, and you should not have sex before getting married. Some cultures believe that this makes for mutual respect, faithfulness and true love.

Other couples believe sex and intimacy is an important part of their relationship and believe they're mature enough to handle it. It just depends on you, your circumstances, and how much you feel for the other person. There is plenty of exploring of each other's bodies which can be enjoyed without having to 'go all the way' and have full penetrative sex.

Source: *But You Don't Understand*, by Elaine Sishton and Charlotte Russell

In groups

1 What do you think of these reasons for having sex? Discuss each one in turn.

2 Some people think the age of consent should be lowered from 16 to 14. Discuss the arguments for and against.

"I'm worried s/he will leave me if I don't agree."

"We've discussed it and it's something we both want to do."

"Everyone else is doing it."

"When I'm drunk, I can't stop myself. I'll do anything with anyone."

"I just want to find out what it's like."

Sex = love?

Sex is not the same thing as love in the true sense of the word. Sex can be self-centred and a purely physical craving. There are people who see the opposite sex as just 'bodies' to be used. Don't deceive yourself into thinking that people really care for you if all they want is sex. The truth is that they may not care for you as much as you would like. Hormones are flying high in the teenage years, and people feel they want to experiment.

There is a lot of pressure and gossip among groups as to who has 'done it', when, and with whom. Boys in particular may try to blackmail girls into having sex, and try every trick and persuasive argument they can think of. Don't be conned into doing something you may later regret. Respect yourself and your own body. Take no notice of pressure from other people – it is your decision alone.

Protection

If you do decide an active sex life is right for you, then there are a few important things to consider. The main one is risk. Pregnancy or sexually transmitted infections (STIs), such as genital herpes or chlamydia, are real dangers to be considered. Protect yourself by:

- not having sex
- avoiding situations that you may find it difficult to get out of, such as getting drunk at a party and not being able to think clearly
- sticking to one partner (the more partners you have, the more chance you have of catching a sexually transmitted infection)
- using condoms (although not 100% safe, these significantly reduce the dangers).

Source: *But You Don't Understand*, by Elaine Sishton and Charlotte Russell

Resisting pressure

You can resist all kinds of pressure if you give your own preferences priority.

"It's very easy to have sex, but I want more than that."

"I know you've got your values, but I've got mine, and they're important to me."

"It's childish not to consider the consequences of having sex."

"An orgasm isn't everything."

Source: *Sex Ed*, by Dr Miriam Stoppard

⠿ In groups

1 Discuss how you would explain to a partner that being in love doesn't mean you have to have sex. How would you say 'No'?

2 How helpful do you find the responses Dr Miriam Stoppard suggests? Can you suggest any other responses?

Safer sex and contraception

Practising safer sex

Aim To understand methods of contraception and how to practise safer sex, and to discuss unplanned pregnancies (Personal wellbeing 1.2a, 1.3a, 1.3b, 1.3c, 2.2a, 2.2b, 2.2c, 3d, 3e)

What is safer sex?

All sex involves some risk. That's why people refer to 'safer' sex rather than 'safe' sex. Practising safer sex means taking precautions to protect yourself against an unplanned pregnancy or catching a sexually transmitted infection (STI). It means avoiding risky sexual practices that could harm you, either physically or emotionally.

THE LOWDOWN ON...
contraception

If you're considering having sex, you need to think about contraception first. The most popular forms of contraception for young people are condoms and the Pill. There are also female condoms and hormone injections, which should be discussed with your GP.

Condoms

When placed over a hard penis, condoms trap sperm when a boy ejaculates. They're 98% effective against pregnancy and can protect against STIs. Look for condoms with the CE and British kitemark symbols; use them once only and note the expiry date. Oil-based products (baby oil and Vaseline) can damage condoms, as can nails or jewellery.

The Pill

There are two types – the mini pill (containing the hormone progestogen) and the combined pill (containing oestrogen and progestogen). The Pill is 99% effective against pregnancy but it does not protect against STIs.

Emergency contraception (morning-after pill)

If a contraceptive method fails, emergency contraception pills can help. They can be used up to 72 hours after sex, but the sooner they're taken, the better. The pills are available free from GPs, family planning clinics, Brook Centres and NHS walk-in centres. They are also available from pharmacies (for over 16s) and cost £24. However, they should be used only as a last resort – you shouldn't have sex because you know that you can get the morning-after pill.

In groups

"The morning-after pill should be available in all schools confidentially to anyone who asks for it, whatever their age."

1 Discuss the arguments for and against this view, and say why you agree or disagree with it.

2 In a few years' time it may be possible for men to have a hormonal contraceptive implanted under the arm which would last for a year. Do you think men would want to use this method? Who should take responsibility for contraception – the man or the woman?

For your file

"My girlfriend's going on the Pill. Do I still need to use a condom?" K

Draft a reply to K's letter.

76

THE LOWDOWN ON...
pregnancy

Get sussed before you get serious

If you've ever had sex or thought about it, one of your biggest concerns might be the risk of getting pregnant.

First things first. What some girls don't realise is that if sperm come into contact with the vagina in any way, there is a risk of getting pregnant. This means that if a lad has sperm on his fingers he should keep them away from your privates. It is also possible to fall pregnant if you have sex during your period.

The best way to avoid pregnancy is to never have sexual contact without a reliable method of contraception, regardless of the time of the month.

If you miss a period and think you might be pregnant (bear in mind that periods can be erratic in your teens), you should take a pregnancy test as soon as possible. It is important to find out if you're pregnant or not, so that you have time to consider all your options.

What if I'm pregnant?

Facing an unplanned pregnancy is difficult at any age, but can be even more distressing if you're under 16 and may not know what options are available to you. It's common to feel shocked, confused, embarrassed, isolated or lonely when facing an unplanned pregnancy.

Remember – you are not alone. If you feel unable to talk to your family or boyfriend, professionals are there to provide information and support. Once you have been advised of the options, you can make a decision about what's best for you.

The options open to a girl who is under 16 years old and gets pregnant are:

• keep the baby • have the baby adopted • have an abortion.

REAL LIFE

Susie, 19, felt confused and upset when she discovered she was pregnant.

"I was on the Pill when I fell pregnant. No one told me that if you're sick it can affect the Pill and it may not be as effective. After I started getting stomach pains I went to see the doctor, and when he told me I was pregnant I couldn't believe it. My boyfriend burst into tears when I told him, but said he'd stick by whatever decision I made. After professional advice we agreed that having an abortion was best as we felt too young to take on the responsibility of a child.

In December I went to hospital to have the abortion. The doctor gave me a tablet to take and a few days later I went back to be given a pill internally. It wasn't pleasant, but I knew it was the right thing for me. You can never be too careful when it comes to contraception. Prevention is the best thing."

Source: *J17*

For your file

Write an article for a magazine for young people advising teenagers about the options open to them if they become pregnant and what things they need to consider when deciding whether to have the baby or to have an abortion.

In groups

Discuss the options above. What are the key factors that should influence the girl's decision? How much say should the father have? How much say should her parents have? What are the arguments for and against having an abortion?

Understanding why people drink

Aim To discuss why people drink, to understand the risks of binge-drinking, and to explore ways of drinking sensibly (Personal wellbeing 1.2a, 1.3a, 1.3b, 2.2a, 2.2b, 2.2c, 3d, 3e)

Alcohol
– what's the attraction?

Alcohol plays a big part in our world, with over 90% of adults enjoying a drink on a regular basis. That doesn't make it compulsory for you to drink alcohol, but understanding the reasons for its appeal could help you to drink sensibly.

The buzz

Like any drug, alcohol affects your mood. In small amounts, it can help people loosen up, so they feel chatty and less self-conscious. The problems kick in only if you turn to drink because it seems like the only way to have a good time, or because you're uptight, bored or lacking the self-confidence just to be yourself when sober.

The image

OK, so hard drinking has a macho appeal. We're led to believe that a real man can drink without dropping, while our action-movie heroes are often seen steadying their nerves with a drop of the strong stuff. In reality, if you drink to get drunk, the end result is always the same. You might have a good time up to a point, but after that you risk spinning out of control, vomiting or just doing something you badly regret. It doesn't impress, and it won't leave you feeling good about yourself.

Source: *XY: A Toolkit for Life*, by Matt Whyman

GETTING TRASHED
the risks

- You may get alcohol poisoning and end up in hospital. Several teenagers die each year from acute alcohol poisoning or from choking on their own vomit.

- You are more likely to pick an argument and get into a fight.

- You are more likely to have an accident. 40% of visits to hospital casualty departments are drink-related, rising to 70% at weekends.

- You may find yourself having sex with someone you'd rather not have had sex with. You may not use a condom, risking an unwanted pregnancy or STI.

- You may do something stupid and commit a criminal offence.

- Regularly drinking too much means you risk becoming dependent on alcohol.

- Long-term heavy drinkers can damage their livers and develop cirrhosis.

For your file

Dear Erica,
"I am worried about my brother, who's 17. He's started binge-drinking. What are the risks? What can I say to him to get him to stop?" Taz

Write a reply to Taz's letter.

THE RISKS OF BINGE-DRINKING
Put an end to 'happy hours'

The bars that compete with others by offering cheap, reckless promos are not taking their responsibilities as licensees seriously. 'Happy hours' introduce a time pressure to get the best value, and people who get drunk early on tend to continue drinking.

Ban TV adverts 'glorifying' drink, say doctors

Doctors have called for a ban on television advertising of alcohol in an attempt to stem the rising tide of binge-drinking by young people. They say "We all agree that in moderation drinking is a good thing, but adverts don't say 'have a glass or two'. Alcohol harms and we want to see the glorification of it on our television screens ended."

Source: *Daily Telegraph*

Measures to cut down binge-drinking

- Don't allow under 18s into bars after 8pm.
- Ban TV adverts that 'glorify' drink.
- Put health warnings on all alcoholic drinks.
- Ban promotions such as 'happy hours'.
- Increase on-the-spot fines for drunkenness.
- Make young people who are found drunk and disorderly attend alcohol-education classes.

In groups

Discuss the 'Measures to cut down on binge-drinking' on the left. Which do you think would be most effective? What other measures can you suggest?

In groups

"We go out to get wrecked. It's a laugh."

"People who don't drink are killjoys."

"A person who's drunk is a real turn-off."

"There are lots of ways of having a good night out without getting trashed."

1 Discuss the views above. What would you say to someone who said that to you?

2 Plan a video to warn young people of the dangers of binge-drinking. Take turns to present your plans to the rest of the class.

In pairs

Study the information on how to be smart about drinking. Write down the reasons for each piece of advice.

Ways to drink sensibly

Drinking isn't compulsory – you can choose not to booze. Being smart about alcohol means thinking ahead, so here are some tips to be sure that alcohol doesn't get the better of you.

- Eat a decent meal before you go out. Starchy stuff, like bread, potatoes and pasta, and fatty food such as chips, take a while to digest and will help absorb alcohol.
- Aim to enjoy a drink as part of the social setting, but to respect your limits. If you're not sure what you can handle, take it easy. You'll soon learn where to draw the line.
- Pace yourself. Give your body a chance to process the alcohol from one drink to the next. Also sip each drink instead of swigging it down.
- Alternate alcohol with water and a non-alcoholic, non-fizzy drink now and then.
- Avoid mixing drinks. Different types of booze mean more toxins to deal with. As a result you may find you stop enjoying yourself and start wishing you hadn't had that last drink.

Source: *XY: A Toolkit for Life*, by Matt Whyman

Aim To understand how smoking and passive smoking can damage your health, and to discuss techniques that can be used to resist unhelpful pressure to smoke or drink (Personal wellbeing 1.2a, 1.3a, 1.3b, 2.2a, 2.2b, 2.2c, 2.2d, 3d, 3e)

Smoking – what's the attraction?

The smoking lifestyle

Lighting up is often viewed as an act of rebellion, and even sophistication. It's a strong image used by the cigarette industry and media to reinforce certain ideas, attitudes and beliefs.

Joining the pack

Peer pressure can be a powerful force, which means that if your mates are lighting up, then you might find it hard to resist. Much depends on your self-esteem – if you feel confident in yourself, then you are less likely to smoke.

Mood control

Nicotine in tobacco is a powerful and fast-acting drug that has a stimulating effect on the body. Even so, many people believe that reaching for the cigarettes helps them stay calm, relieving stress and feelings of nervousness.

Source: *XY: A Toolkit for Life*, by Matt Whyman

The risks

Lighting up

- 90% of deaths from lung cancer are linked to smoking. It also causes 80% of the deaths from diseases such as bronchitis, emphysema and heart disease.

- A person who smokes is likely to die between six and nine years younger than a non-smoker.

- Research suggests that 120,000 men under 50 are sexually impotent because of smoking.

- Tobacco can stain your teeth and nails, make your skin wrinkled and your breath smell. The smoke gets into your hair and clothes and makes them smell, too.

- Around 5,000 fires a year are caused by smoking-related materials, resulting in about 160 deaths.

Passive smoking

- The immediate effects of passive smoking include eye irritation, headache, cough, sore throat, dizziness and feeling sick. Other people's smoke can reduce coronary blood flow.

- 80% of asthma sufferers say tobacco smoke causes them to have breathing difficulties.

- 17,000 children under five go into hospital each year as a result of their parents' smoking.

- Non-smokers who are exposed to passive smoking at home have a 25% increased risk of heart disease and lung cancer.

- It is estimated that 1,000 people die each year as a result of diseases caused by passive smoking.

RESISTING THE PRESSURE TO SMOKE
Erica Stewart offers some tips on how to say 'No'

Saying 'No' isn't easy. Don't feel you have to give a long explanation of why you don't want to smoke (or have a drink). Try a few of the responses below.

Don't get drawn into a discussion or an argument, try to change the conversation. Remember, a true friend will respect you enough to accept what you're saying and to leave it to you to make your own decisions, instead of trying to get you to do what they want you to do.

In groups

1 Discuss how some people put pressure on others to either smoke or drink. What sort of things do they say? How would you say 'No'?

2 How helpful do you find the responses Erica Stewart suggests? Can you suggest any other responses?

"No, thanks."

"I just don't feel in the mood for it today."

"I don't need one right now."

"I'm in training at the moment."

"If I smoke, it makes me feel ill."

"I've tried it and I don't like it."

"I get an allergic reaction if I have one."

"I've been told not to because of a condition I have."

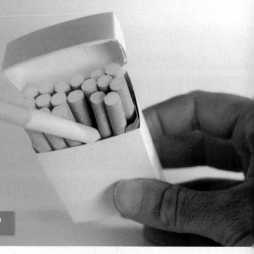

In groups

"Health warnings on cigarette packets are a waste of time. No one takes any notice."

"The only way to cut down the number of smokers is to raise the price of cigarettes to a level where people can't afford to buy them."

"People have a right to smoke if they want to. No one should be able to dictate to you where you can or cannot smoke."

1 Discuss the views above.

2 Some doctors have called for a total ban on the sale of tobacco. The director of ASH (Action for Smoking and Health) says such a ban is 'neither possible, nor desirable'. What do you think?

3 Imagine you are one of a team of advisers appointed by the government to draw up plans for an anti-smoking campaign aimed at teenagers. Draw up your plans and present them to the rest of the class.

For your file

Dear Erica
"My boyfriend smokes and tells me not to be ridiculous when I say it affects me, too. What can I say to him? I'm afraid if I challenge him, he'll dump me." Gaby

Draft a reply to Gaby's letter.

Keeping healthy

Aim To understand how to take responsibility for your own health
(Personal wellbeing 1.2a, 1.2b, 1.3a, 2.2a, 2.2b, 2.2c, 3e, 4h)

Looking after your own health

As a young adult, you will be beginning to take responsibility for your own healthcare. The more you know about your health, the more you will have the power to make your own choices about how to look after yourself. Below are some of the things it is useful to know:

1 GP's details: the name, address and telephone number of your doctor

2 National health card/NHS number and where you keep them

3 Immunisations: what you have had and where you keep your immunisation record card

4 Illnesses: what illnesses you have had, e.g. mumps, measles, chicken pox, German measles

5 Allergies: anything you are allergic to, e.g. medicines, plasters, foods, and how to deal with it

6 Medical conditions: details of any medical conditions you may have and any medication you take, e.g. dosage, side effects

7 Family history: any medical conditions that are common in your family, e.g. high blood pressure, diabetes

8 Accidents and emergencies: addresses of the nearest hospitals with a walk-in centre for minor injuries and with an Accident and Emergency department

● On your own

Look at the checklist above. How many of the details listed do you know? Create your own checklist and do some research to fill in any gaps.

Immunisations

Immunisations give you vaccines that will protect you from catching certain highly infectious diseases.

Have you had your booster vaccine which tops up your immunity protection against tetanus, diphtheria and polio? It is available to all young people aged between 13 and 18.

A new vaccine – the HPV vaccine – provides protection against the virus that causes 70% of cases of cervical cancer. Routine vaccination for girls aged 12–13 was introduced in September 2008. In 2010/11 it is to be offered to all 15–16 year old girls, as part of a catch-up programme.

In pairs

Discuss why it is important to keep yourself fit and healthy by taking regular exercise. Design a website page offering advice on fun ways of taking exercise and keeping fit.

NHS Direct

NHS Direct provides health advice and information 24 hours a day, 365 days a year, both online and on the phone.

- You can check your symptoms and get personalised advice online at www.nhsdirect.nhs.uk

- You can phone NHS Direct on 0845 46 47 for advice when you are ill or on any health issue.

- You can use the self-help guide to get advice on how to treat common problems at home.

During the swine flu epidemic in 2009, NHS Direct played an important role in providing patients with medication, because people with flu were advised to stay away from their doctors' surgeries, so as not to infect other people.

For your file

One in three people in the UK suffers from an allergy. Use the NHS Direct website to find out about allergies. Focus on one particular allergy, such as hayfever, and design a poster offering advice on what to do to alleviate the symptoms. Further information can be found at www.allergyuk.org – the website of the charity Allergy UK.

Dealing with minor ailments

Lots of minor ailments can be self-treated safely and effectively with advice and medicine from a pharmacy.

Minor ailments are those that don't pose a serious threat to health, and some clear up on their own. They include:

- bugs and viruses – coughs, colds, flu, cold sores, sore throats
- sports injuries such as minor cuts and bruises, sprains and strains
- stomach problems – indigestion, diarrhoea, constipation
- women's health – candida (thrush), period pains
- skin conditions – spots, dandruff, athlete's foot, corns, warts and veruccas
- allergies – contact dermatitis, hay fever
- aches and pains – headache, toothache.

Pharmacists have the expertise to help you choose and use medicines to deal with minor ailments. There are over-the-counter medicines that you can buy from the pharmacy without a prescription like aspirins and antacids. Many common ailments, such as colds and flu, can be self-treated without the need for a doctor's prescription.

Source: 'Head for your pharmacy', Doctor Patient Partnership

In pairs

Discuss how a pharmacy can help you to deal with minor ailments.

Healthcare check

Aim To examine the health risks of sunbathing, tattooing and body piercing (Personal wellbeing 1.2a, 1.3a, 2.2a, 2.2b, 2.2c, 3d, 4h)

Sunbathing
– is it worth the risk?

Young people in Britain will face a skin cancer 'time bomb' unless they heed warnings about exposure to the sun and stop their obsessive pursuit of tans, say health experts.

A survey of 16- and 24-year-olds found that more than 70% of them wanted a tan on holiday, despite the risk of potentially fatal skin cancer from ultraviolet (UV) radiation. It is important for young people to change their habits and learn to protect themselves properly in the sun.

A burning problem

- There are almost 70,000 cases of skin cancer in Britain every year, the most deadly form of which is malignant melanoma. This form causes around 1,700 deaths a year.
- As a result of a 20-year campaign in Australia, the country has about 1,000 skin cancer deaths a year – 700 fewer than Britain
- Getting a tan by 'binge' sunbathing at weekends or on a two-week holiday abroad significantly increases the risk of getting skin cancer.

Sun protection tips

- **Stay in the shade between 11am and 3pm.**
- **Make sure you never burn.**
- **Cover up with a T-shirt, wide-brimmed hat and sunglasses.**
- **Use factor 15-plus sunscreen.**

Melanoma – the facts

- Skin cancers are caused by the ultraviolet radiation (UV) in the sun's rays, which can damage the DNA in your cells.
- A melanoma develops as a new mole that is black or odd-looking, or as an old mole that has changed.
- In men, the most common area for melanomas to appear is on the torso; in women, it is on the legs.
- Malignant melanomas are treatable. They can be surgically removed – an operation that leaves hardly any scarring.

⠿ In groups

1 Discuss what you have learned about the dangers of sunbathing. Why is 'binge sunbathing' so risky?

2 Design a poster to warn teenagers of the risks of sunbathing and to give them advice on things they can do to reduce the risks.

● On your own

Find out more about the prevention, diagnosis and treatment of melanoma from the following website: www.melanoma.com/melanoma/index.jsp

TATTOOS

Tattoos are permanent. That's because the tattooist uses a needle to inject coloured ink deep into your skin. Once it's done, you have to live with it – a tattoo won't wear off. That's why it's illegal to tattoo someone under the age of 18.

If you want a tattoo, only go to a licensed tattoo parlour as tattoos must be given under totally hygienic conditions. If the needles aren't sterile, there's a risk of being infected with conditions such as tetanus or HIV.

Surveys show that 75% of people who have a tattoo eventually regret it and seek advice about how to get it removed. It is possible to remove tattoos by laser treatment, but it is very expensive. So think twice before you get a tattoo!

In pairs

Discuss why you think tattoos are so popular. What reasons are there against having a permanent tattoo? What health risks are there from having a temporary tattoo?

For your file

Write an article for a teenage magazine entitled: 'Think twice before you get a tattoo'.

Temporary tattoos

Temporary henna tattoos are very fashionable, but they too can lead to health problems. Skin specialists say that the henna goes beneath the epidermis (top layer of skin) and can cause irritation.

Never have a black henna tattoo. This is because a chemical called PPD is sometimes added to pure henna to make black henna. PPD is black hair dye and should be used only in a very diluted form or there's a risk that it could leave an unsightly scar.

"I wanted to show my independence, so I got my ears and eyebrow pierced." Max

"My mates all had piercings, so I got some. It's no big deal." Jo

"I did it 'cause it's fashionable." Paul

"I had it done for a dare to impress my boyfriend." Min

Body piercing

Body piercing is increasingly popular. There's no age limit for getting pierced, but it must be done by someone who's been trained and who uses sterilised equipment. You should also weigh up the health risks, which include infections, bleeding and skin damage.

In groups

1 Why do you think body piercing has become so popular? What do you think are the main reasons why people get their bodies pierced?

2 "Body piercing should be as strictly controlled as tattooing." Say why you agree or disagree with this view.

Assessing your skills and investigating careers

Aim To begin thinking about careers, based on an assessment of your personal skills (Economic wellbeing and financial capability 1.1a, 1.1b, 1.1c, 1.2c, 2.1a, 2.1b, 2.1c, 2.1d, 2.2a, 2.3a, 2.3c, 3e, 3f, 4f, 4h)

Which career?

Hundreds of careers and only one lifetime – how on earth do you decide what's best for you? Maybe you're one of the lucky ones: you know what you want, and you know exactly what's needed to get there.

Don't worry if you're unsure or a bit confused about all the choices. Probably half the population already working would say they're equally unsure or confused about what they want to do!

Nowadays many people totally change career direction two, three, or even more times in their lives. So if you do start off in the 'wrong' job, there's nothing to stop you changing later on. If you're flexible and willing to re-train where necessary, you're laughing!

Source: www.prospects.co.uk/careers

Start with yourself

Knowing more about yourself will help you choose a career that is likely to suit you. Follow these steps:

1 Write down:
- something your best friend likes about you
- something your parents/carers say is good about you
- something your parents/carers criticise about you
- something good that your tutor has written or said is good about you
- something your tutor is always asking you to improve.

2 Then write down:
- your best quality
- something you think you need to improve
- a recent achievement you are proud of
- something you wish you'd done better.

3 Discuss what you have written with a partner. Adjust as necessary.

4 Finally, write a statement about yourself that describes your strengths and the areas for improvement. Can you suggest some careers that may suit someone with your strengths and weaknesses?

Source: *Step Three 2003–4*

Skills 4 Jobs

Skills can be divided into five main areas:

1 People skills:

- communication
- inspiration
- negotiation
- delegation
- advising

2 Thinking skills:

- evaluating
- problem solving
- proritising
- weighing up evidence and alternatives

3 Using information:

- memorising
- researching
- calculating
- organising
- observing

4 Helping people get things done:

- coordinating and liaising
- overseeing
- planning
- recognising other people's talents and skills

5 Seeing things from a different angle:

- finding alternatives
- thinking laterally
- flair and imagination
- seeing potential
- finding links

Source: adapted from *Your Future*

Job families

There are so many jobs available that sometimes it is easier to break them down into job families. The list below gives some job families and what they involve.

- **Scientific** – finding out why and how things work, applying science
- **Social service** – helping people with problems, caring for them
- **Literary** – using the written or spoken word
- **Artistic** – applying a creative skill in art, design, music or drama
- **General service** – providing a service to the public
- **Mechanical** – making, using or repairing machinery
- **Natural** – working with plants, animals and other natural resources
- **Numerical** – working with figures or solving mathematical problems
- **Practical** – being directly involved in making products
- **Driving** – driving a vehicle
- **Outdoor/active** – being out and about, and physically active

Source: *Options at 16+*, a Connexions Gloucestershire publication

In pairs

1 Look at the list of skills in the article 'Skills 4 Jobs'. Discuss what skills you think you have. Choose four or five skills from the list.

2 Now look at the list of job families. What kinds of job would make the best use of your skills?

3 Find some job adverts in local or national newspapers. Which jobs would you be most interested in? Do you feel your skills fit these jobs best?

For your file

Choose a career that interests you. Use the Internet and careers library, and talk to people already doing this job. Write a report, including what activities you would do, where you would work and with whom, how much you would earn, and what skills and qualifications you would need.

Aim To begin thinking about your work placement, and to consider the importance of health and safety at work (Economic wellbeing and financial capability 1.1a, 1.1b, 1.1c, 2.1c, 2.1d, 2.3a, 2.3c, 3c, 3f, 4a, 4b, 4c, 4d)

Preparing for
work experience

Why bother with work experience?

Don't let the phrase 'work experience' fill you with fear. It's a way of exploring the world of work – from the inside. Whether it is in a factory, a hospital or an office, a work placement could help you to get a job when you leave school.

Taking part in a work placement will benefit you in a variety of ways:

- You will learn what it is really like going to work every day and doing a job.
- Your team-working, time-keeping and communication skills will all benefit.
- You will practise using your initiative (and asking for help, should you need it).
- You may even end up with a job, if you work hard and impress your boss.

Some time during Year 10 you will go on a work-experience placement. The activities on this spread are designed to prepare you for this and to help you get the most out of it.

Case study:
Jas – in the shadows

Jas has always wanted to be a solicitor, so she was pleased that she was going to a solicitor's on work experience. On her placement she visited the law courts and the local police station. However, most of her time was spent in the office where she researched information and carried out clerical work, such as photocopying. She also shadowed (followed) a solicitor, who spent most of his time reading, writing letters and talking to clients on the telephone. She felt law was not as glamorous as she had thought – there was too much paperwork!

Case study:
Mark – a cut above

Mark does not know what he wants to do when he leaves school. Teachers think he is shy, lacking in confidence, and not always reliable.

He didn't care where he went for work experience. The only placement left was at the local hairdresser. Mark had to talk to customers, wash their hair, sweep the floor, make cups of tea, and take telephone bookings. He turned up on time every day and enjoyed chatting to customers in the shop and on the phone. The hairdressers were very impressed with him and have offered him a part-time job in the school holidays.

Source: Jackie Reynolds

In groups

1 Discuss the reasons you have for doing work experience.

2 What particular skills – either personal or practical – do you want to practise or develop?

3 From the two case studies, what do you think Jas and Mark learned from their work experience?

Health and safety

As you get older, you need to start taking more responsibility for yourself and for other people. It's important to be aware of health and safety issues, especially when you are on a work placement and are less experienced than those around you.

THE LAW

According to the Health and Safety at Work Act, employers must:

- maintain safe systems of work
- ensure the safe use, handling, storage and transport of articles and substances
- provide adequate instruction, training and supervision
- maintain safe premises and a safe working environment.

And employees must:

- take reasonable care of their own health and safety, and that of others
- cooperate with their employers and others
- not interfere with or misuse anything provided to protect their health and safety, e.g. equipment and protective clothing.

THE FACTS

- Thousands of young people have accidents at work every year. Some of them are fatal.
- According to the Trade Union Congress, 10 young workers are seriously injured at work every week because they are not aware of their basic health and safety rights as employees, and have not been given adequate training by their employers.
- Many injuries result from contact with moving machinery, moving objects (including vehicles), and while handling, lifting and carrying things (manual handling).

In groups

1 What is meant by 'safe systems of work'? Can you give an example?

2 Do you think employers should take responsibility for health and safety at work, or the employee? Or should it be shared equally? Give reasons for your views.

In pairs

Look at the list of occupations below.

- garage mechanic
- hairdresser
- gardener
- shop assistant.

For each job, list some health and safety issues you think you should be aware of if you were a) the employer, and b) the employee.

For your file

Think about your own work experience placement. Write a paragraph stating health and safety risks you should be concerned about, and what precautions you should take.

For your file

When you have chosen a placement and completed an application form, you will need to send a covering letter. Write a paragraph on:

- why you think work experience is important,
- what you can offer the placement,
- why you think you should be offered the placement.

Getting started on work experience

Work experience ESSENTIALS

Aim To prepare yourself in more detail for your work placement (Economic wellbeing and financial capability 1.1a, 1.1b, 1.1c, 2.1a, 2.1b, 2.1d, 2.3a, 2.3c, 3c, 3f, 4a, 4b, 4c, 4d)

Before your placement

Think about, and then note down, what you can offer on your placement, and what you'd like to achieve. Then carry out some research. Try to answer the following questions:

- What does your chosen company do?
- How big is it?
- What kinds of jobs do the people working there do?
- What are the working hours?
- What should you wear? Will you need special clothing or can you just dress smartly?
- How will you get there? How long will the journey take and how much will it cost?
- Will you need to take your own lunch or is there a canteen? How much money will you need to take with you for lunch?
- Work out how much money you will need for transport and food every day.

During your placement

There are some simple things to remember when on your placement, whether you decide you'd like to work for that particular company in the future or not:

- Be polite and considerate. Remember, you never know when you'll meet someone you were rude to again. They might be interviewing you for a job in a few years' time!
- Arrive on time and leave only when you are supposed to.
- Try to avoid sitting doing nothing. If you have time to spare, offer to help someone else.
- Make sure you are keen and helpful, and take care not to join in with office gossip.
- Dress appropriately. If you are in an office you will probably need to wear smart clothes. Other jobs may require you to tie back your hair, to remove/cover ear or nose studs, or to wear protective clothing.
- Don't forget to smile!

Finally, remember that work experience is there to help you – so watch your colleagues, learn from them and don't be afraid to ask questions. Even if the job is not the one for you, it will offer you lots of experiences that will help you decide what you want to do in the future.

After your placement

- Write down what you've learned and the training you've received. Include how you managed your time and your workload, and how you overcame any problems. Include this summary on your progress file and/or CV.
- Ask for detailed feedback from your supervisor and ask them if they'll be a reference on your CV.
- Keep in touch with the people you've met – they can let you know about other opportunities in the future.

In groups

1 Discuss what you have learned about work experience essentials.

2 Which are the most useful pieces of advice? Compile a group list of five top tips and share it with the class, giving your reasons.

The employer's report

When you have finished your work experience, your employer will report back to the school, using a form like the one below. The information in this report will go into your Progress File, so it is important to achieve the best report possible.

Work Experience Employer's Report

Student Name: *Angela Butt* **Form:** *10W* **Placement name:** *Touchwood Sports Ltd*

Placement address: *High Street, Mansfield*

Competences: Please indicate student competences using levels 1 to 4:

1 = competent without help	2 = competent with some help	3 = competent with a great deal of help given	4 = cannot cope at present	N/A = not applicable

a	Responding appropriately with clients	2	**i**	Following instructions	3
b	Responding appropriately with supervisor	1	**j**	Following tasks through to the end	3
c	Responding appropriately with colleagues	2	**k**	Making independent decisions, showing initiative	2
d	Dealing constructively with criticism	4	**l**	Demonstrating appropriate attendance and punctuality	1
e	Working with others (teamwork)	4	**m**	Demonstrating dependability	2
f	Working alone	2	**n**	Dealing with problems	2
g	Demonstrating appropriate appearance and manner	1	**o**	Asking questions when in doubt	3
h	Demonstrating interest and enthusiasm	1	**p**	Learning new things	2

Please give an overview of the student's achievements

....

....

....

....

Name: *Valerie Childs* **Position:** *Supervisor* **Date:** *3/5/09*

 **In pairs**

Read Angela's work experience progress report above. Discuss how well she has done on her placement. What are her strengths and weaknesses? What advice would you give her?

For your file

Think of your own work experience placement. Which of the areas on the work experience report do you think you will find difficult? What could you do about these areas to make sure you get a good report from your employer? Write a paragraph detailing your thoughts.

Aim To understand the importance of budgeting and how to plan a budget (Economic wellbeing and financial capability 1.2b, 2.4a, 3h)

"It's not important."

"I'll worry about it tomorrow."

"I've got no idea where to start."

"It's too scary to look at."

In pairs

Discuss the fears that teenagers have about managing their money. Do you have the same fears or different ones?

School leavers can't budget

Today's typical school leavers know the cost of a computer game but have no idea how to budget for food, rent and bills, according to new research published today.

In a worrying reflection of teenagers' priorities, 26% believe that when they eventually flee the family nest, one of their three biggest expenses will be the cost of going out. 24% believe that clothes will absorb the bulk of their budget, and 20% cite expenditure on their mobile phone bills. Nearly 31% say they are worried about eventually getting into debt.

The survey of 15- and 16-year-old school leavers reveals that 85% know the average cost of a DVD, 80% of a computer game, and 83% of a can of cola. However, 75% don't know the cost of a colour TV licence and 49% estimate that a new basic fridge would cost more than £200.

Source: a report by Rebecca Smithers, www.EducationGuardian.co.uk

Allowances

An allowance is an important stepping stone between the pocket money that you received as a child and the student grant or wage that you will have to manage when you leave school.

The first thing you have to do is to negotiate with your parents over how much allowance you should have and what it should cover.

The more items you are expected to pay for, the bigger your allowance should be. If, after a couple of months, you are really struggling to make ends meet, don't be afraid to go back to your parents and renegotiate.

☐ Books and magazines
☐ CDs
☐ Clothes
☐ Computer games
☐ Films concerts, etc.
☐ Food/drink (when out)
☐ Going out with friends
☐ Hobbies/sports equipment
☐ Make-up/ toiletries
☐ Phone top-ups
☐ Presents
☐ Savings
☐ Sweets
☐ Travel

In groups

1 Are you surprised at the findings in the news article 'School leavers can't budget'? How much does (a) a colour TV licence, (b) a basic fridge, cost?

2 Discuss what you think the three biggest expenses will be when you leave home.

In groups

1 Discuss the advantages and disadvantages of having a monthly rather than weekly allowance.

2 Design a questionnaire to find out the views of students in your class on allowances. For example, ask: Do you have an allowance? How much is it? What does it cover?

How to budget

Hopeless at managing your money? Colin Letts helps you out...

IF YOU ARE WONDERING why you are always running out of money before the end of the week, then the chances are that you are not budgeting properly. (It could also be that you don't have enough money in the first place, in which case you could ask your parents for a bigger allowance or get a Saturday job!)

Budgeting is a fancy word for taking control of your own finances. You do this by calculating, over a set period of time, the following:

- how much money you earn (called income)
- how much money you spend (called outgoings or expenditure)
- how much money you save.

Your first attempt at a budget could look like Figure 1.

If it does, you're in trouble! The totals for columns B and C – the money you are either spending or saving – come to £36 altogether. This is £11 more than your income (column A). To balance your budget, you must either increase your income or decrease the amount you spend or save.

You could decide to postpone starting karate lessons and begin saving for them. You could also reduce your 'other savings' slightly and spend a bit less on going out. Your budget would then look like Figure 2.

The totals for your outgoings and savings (columns B and C) now equal your income (column A), so your budget is balanced.

| Figure 1 | A | B | C |
Item	Weekly income (£)	Weekly outgoings (£)	Savings (£)
Allowance/pocket money	10		
Paper round	15		
Karate lessons		7	
Going out		10	
Saving for clothes			5
Food and drink		5	
Phone top-ups, etc.		4	
Other savings			5
TOTALS	25	26	10

| Figure 2 | A | B | C |
Item	Weekly income (£)	Weekly outgoings (£)	Savings (£)
Allowance/pocket money	10		
Paper round	15		
Karate lessons			2
Going out		8	
Saving for clothes			3
Food and drink		5	
Phone top-ups, etc.		4	
Other savings			3
TOTALS	25	17	8

If you follow this method and keep a regular account of how you spend your money, you will be able to manage your finances. Otherwise they will manage you.

For your file

"I get a really good allowance from my parents, but it never seems to last more than a couple of weeks. I'm always asking them for more money, which irritates them, and I never know what I'm going to be able to afford." Chris, 16

Write a reply to Chris, advising him on how to manage his money better.

In pairs

Work out three other ways in which the budget above could have been balanced. Which is the best way and why? Be prepared to present your conclusions to the rest of the class.

Aim To understand what bank accounts are, what advantages they have and how bank accounts and plastic cards work (Economic wellbeing and financial capability 1.2b, 2.4a, 2.4b, 2.4c, 2.4d, 3h)

Bank accounts and saving

Why do I need a bank account?

Banks and building societies offer a variety of different accounts. Nearly everyone needs an account to help them manage their day-to-day money. It is possible to manage your money using just cash, but putting your money in a bank account can have several advantages.

Bank accounts are safe and convenient. They can help you to:

● **pay bills** – regular payments that you have to make, e.g. electricity bills, can be paid automatically from your bank account by direct debit

● **manage your money** – when your money is in the bank you are less tempted to spend it on impulse. Regular statements allow you to keep track of your income and expenditure

● **receive money** – cheques can be paid directly into your account. This is often how wages, student loans and benefits are paid

● **keep your money safe** – cash can easily be lost or stolen

● **earn interest** – add a small percentage onto the amount in your account

What kind of bank account should I have?

The two main sorts of bank account are:

1 **Current accounts** – suitable for managing your day-to-day finances
2 **Savings accounts** – better for longer term savings.

Current accounts

As banks don't let people under the age of 18 borrow money, you will probably be offered a basic current account. Even if you are older, this type of current account is a good idea if you find it difficult to control your spending.

If you're not careful, you could spend more money than you have in your bank account. This is called going overdrawn; effectively you are borrowing from the bank.

Savings accounts

A savings account is for your spare cash, so that you can save it up and earn a higher rate of interest. But you can't use it for spending, so you won't get a cheque book or plastic card.

You will still be able to withdraw the money if you really have to, but you will probably then lose some of the extra interest.

Source: *Young Citizens' Passport*

Features of a basic bank account

- **A cash card** – so you can take money out at a cash machine, but you can't withdraw more than you have in your account.
- **A Solo or Electron debit card** – which you can use to pay for things in many shops, by phone and over the Internet. With some debit cards, like Solo and Electron, your account is checked before each transaction and goes ahead only if there is enough in your account to meet the payment.
- **Direct debits** – which enable regular bills to be paid automatically direct from your account.
- **Direct credits** – which enable regular payments (such as wages or your student loan) to be paid direct into your account automatically.

Source: www.fsa.gov.uk/consumer/teaching/index.html

Plastic *your flexible friend*

You're in town and Byrite are having a massive sale. You need cash quickly, but didn't bring enough out. What you need is a way of getting money out of your bank without the hassle of filling in forms. You need 'plastic'!

Since you were little, you've probably wanted one – whether it's to prevent you from keeping your money under the bed or to make your wallet/purse look a little more impressive. However, there are several types of plastic banking cards that serve different purposes – some for plain cash withdrawal from machines, or others for ordering that full set of *Top Gear* DVDs off the Internet.

- **Cash card**: This allows you to withdraw cash from a 'hole in the wall' or ATM (Automated Teller Machine).
- **Cheque guarantee card**: If you want to pay for goods by cheque from your current account, you'll probably need one of these to back up your cheque. (The use of cheques has declined dramatically in recent years, and they are likely to be phased out altogether by 2018.)
- **Debit card**: This allows you to make a payment directly from your account. It has largely replaced the combined cheque and cheque guarantee card payment method, and it can also be used as a cash card.
- **Charge card**: Any store card is usually a charge card. You get a set limit and you have to pay off a minimum amount towards it each month.
- **Credit card:** Credit cards allow you to spend money that you don't have, without any interest being charged on it for a certain length of time. However, if you don't pay your credit-card bill in time, the interest on your 'borrowed' money will go up and cost you more. That's why you usually have to be over 18 or 21 before you get one.

Source: Pupiline

In pairs

What are the advantages of opening a bank account? Which do you think are the three most important reasons, and why?

In groups

Discuss reasons you may have for saving money. Think of short-term and long-term reasons, and include saving 'for a rainy day', as well as for planned items or events.

For your file

A friend has gone overdrawn on their current account, but has plenty of money in a savings account. Write a letter to them advising what they should do, including ways to avoid going overdrawn on their current account.

In pairs

Discuss what you have learned about managing your finances. Write a short definition for each of the following:

- current account
- savings account
- cheque book
- debit card
- interest
- cashpoint machine.

Aim To understand why businesses need money and how they obtain it (Economic wellbeing and financial capability 1.3a, 1.3b, 1.4a, 1.4b, 3g, 3j, 4a, 4g).

Why businesses need money

Businesses need money for several different reasons.

- Firstly, in order to set up a business, you may need to buy materials and equipment, rent premises, and set up an office or factory. These are known as the assets that are required to run a business.

- Secondly, a business needs money in order to survive. The money coming into a business needs to be more than the money going out, otherwise the business will lose money and eventually fail.

- Finally, businesses may need money to buy more assets in order to expand.

Case Study: Graceful Hair

Grace trained as a hairdresser, and worked for several years at a salon in the centre of the city where she lived. She always wanted to have a business of her own, so she saved some money towards the cost of setting up her own studio.

She drew up a business plan and applied to her bank for a loan. She also found that she was entitled to a government grant, which was available at that time for people starting up small businesses in her local area.

Having found premises to rent and bought the necessary equipment, Grace opened her own hairdressing business which she called Graceful Hair. The business prospered, and after a few years, Grace was able to take out another bank loan and open a second studio.

In groups

1. Explain the reasons why businesses need money and how it can be raised privately. Discuss how Grace raised the money to set up her hairdressing studios.

2. Discuss the views on the right.

"I'd never invest in a business. It's too risky. I prefer to keep my money in a savings account where it's safe."

"The rewards of investing in businesses can be much greater than just putting your money in a savings account. I'm prepared to take the risk."

Private financing

Many businesses are financed privately. People invest money in the business in the hope that it will make a profit. If the business is successful, their money will be safe and they will share the rewards of its success. However, they risk losing their money if the business fails.

Private financing includes loans from banks. The loan will have to be repaid over a set period of time. You also have to pay interest on the loan.

Another way of raising money privately is to sell shares in the business - a company can sell off parts of itself, known as shares. The shares of big companies are listed on the Stock Exchange in London. Shares can be bought and sold. When a company is profitable, the shares pay out some money to shareholders, known as dividends. If a company fails and becomes bankrupt, then its shares become worthless.

If a business is successful, it may fund its expansion from its own sales income by keeping some of its profit, and re-investing it at a later date. For example, Grace used some of the profits made by her first studio to pay for the cost of opening her second studio.

Public financing

Public financing means government financing through the Department of Business or the Department of Employment, which seek to support businesses.

Support may take the form of:

- A public loan – a low cost loan to help a business to grow and expand, supporting the local economy. This costs less due to a lower rate of interest that the Government can guarantee.

- A government grant – a grant may be available to encourage people to set up businesses in deprived areas with high levels of unemployment.

For your file

Research the Department of Business and/or the Department of Employment on the Internet. Prepare a short presentation, summarising what they do. Deliver this presentation to the rest of the class.

What sort of finance is best for my business?

When a business chooses to raise some money, it has to consider several different questions:

How much money do we need to raise?

↓

Can we get any of this money for free, in the form of government grants?

↓

How much would we need to borrow?

↓

How long do we need to borrow the money for?

↓

What terms and conditions will apply to borrowing the money?

↓

How are we going to pay the money back?

↓

Would it be better to raise the money by selling shares?

For your file

Imagine you run a small business, such as a florist, a butcher's or a garage and need to raise money for your business. What are the advantages and disadvantages of a bank loan? What are the advantages and disadvantages of selling shares in the business? How would you choose to raise the money? Why? Give reasons for your views.

Aim To understand that running a business involves costs, and that this influences the price charged for goods or services (Economic wellbeing and financial capability 1.4a, 1.4b, 2.3i, 3g, 3j, 4a, 4g)

Fixed costs and variable costs

Costs in business can be put into two groups: fixed and variable.

▲ This removal firm's costs include the cost of buying and running the van, as well as the workers' wages.

▲ It can be expensive to advertise, but the cost needs to be measured against the amount of income generated by the business that the advertisement attracts.

Fixed costs

A fixed cost stays the same however many goods the business produces or services it provides.

Examples of fixed costs include:

- The rent on premises.
- Wages paid to the staff who work for the business.
- Business tax on premises.

Variable costs

A variable cost changes according to the amount of goods or services a business produces. Variable costs can include the following:

- Raw materials used to produce goods and services in the business.
- Heating, lighting and electricity for the business's offices or factories.
- Transport costs.
- Repairs and maintenance of machinery.
- Marketing and advertising for the business.

 **In groups**

'It's always better to set a lower price to make sure you get plenty of work or sell more goods.'

'You mustn't set prices too low, otherwise you won't make enough profit.'

'If you set prices too high, you may not sell enough goods or services and you could go bankrupt.'

Discuss these statements. What do you need to consider when setting prices?

In groups

Imagine you were running a small business such as a cafe, a newsagent's, or a removal firm. Choose a type of business and make lists of your fixed costs and variable costs, then compare them with a partner's lists. How are your costs different from your partner's?

Imagine that the firm employing you is struggling to survive. Your employer asks you to take a pay cut in order to reduce his costs. Discuss the circumstances in which you a) would agree b) would not agree to take it.

Wages

The wages you pay your staff will depend on what sort of work they are doing. You will have to pay a similar amount to that paid to workers in other similar businesses or you may not be able to recruit staff.

You must not discriminate against female members of staff by paying them less than a male worker who is doing exactly the same job. You must pay your staff at least the minimum hourly wage.

Revenue

Revenue is the amount of income a firm receives for the goods it sells or the services it provides. This depends on the prices the firm charges and the amount of goods or services it sells.

Revenue is influenced by how competitive prices are. If you try to undercut your competitors by charging less than them, you may get more work or sell more goods than they do. However, this will not bring in as much revenue as you would get from charging higher prices. So the price you set will affect how much profit you make.

Breaking even

The point at which a business manages to get enough revenue to cover its costs is known as the break-even point. Any revenue from sales beyond this point will generate extra profit. If revenue falls below the break-even point, losses will occur.

Managers use the break-even point as a decision-making tool. For example, a firm selling bicycles will use it to calculate the minimum number of bicycles and other items of cycling equipment it needs to sell, and what price it needs to sell them at in order to make a profit.

Tax

Businesses, like individuals, have to pay tax on the money they make, but only on the profit. All the costs of running the business can be claimed as expenses and do not incur tax.

If a business has annual sales of £68,000 or over, it must register for VAT (Value Added Tax) and must charge VAT on its sales of goods or services. It then has to pay the VAT to the government. However, it can reclaim the VAT charged on any of the costs of running the business. So it is financially beneficial for a business to be registered for VAT.

Aim To understand budgeting and why businesses draw up budget plans (Economic wellbeing and financial capability 1.4a, 1.4b, 2.3i, 3g, 3j, 4a, 4g)

Planning a budget

A budget plan shows how much money a business has, where money will come from in the future, how it will be spent, and how much profit the business hopes to make.

Businesses have a budget plan for several different reasons. A budget enables a business to set targets and to plan for what resources it will need. The various parts of a business budget are often linked. There needs to be a sales budget, because it will affect the production budget. The production budget will affect the budget for raw materials.

For example, if a company budgets to sell 10,000 boxes of chocolates in December, then it will need to budget to produce that number of boxes and to purchase the ingredients required to make that number of chocolates.

A budget will state the targets for a set period of time, for example a year. This means that during the year actual results can be compared with budget figures, and checked to see whether the business is meeting its targets. Managers can also use the budget figures to motivate their staff to hit the targets.

A firm may choose to plan for a longer length of time. For example, they may have a budget for where they expect to be in three or five years' time. Such budgets allow firms to plan how they will grow.

Making adjustments

Sometimes a firm will be forced to alter its budget due to events that are beyond its control, e.g. a rise in the price of petrol or diesel.

In 2008, many firms that had budgeted for a successful year found that, due to the credit crunch, their budgets had to be re-written, and new plans had to be made. Changing a budget is called making an adjustment.

Discuss the reasons why businesses have budget plans. What is an adjustment? Suggest circumstances in which a business might have to make adjustments to its budget.

Types of budgets

An operating budget

This is the day-to-day financial plan for the company. It will include how much cash the company has in its bank, as well as its stock, sales, projected revenue and other costs that make up the day-to-day running of the business.

Summary budgets

These are used to plan activities for different areas of the company over a year. These final accounts will include:

- The profits and losses made by the company during the year.
- A balance sheet which shows where revenue has been generated and where costs have been incurred.
- A cash-flow statement, which shows the financial state of the company month by month.

Marjorie runs a small bakery business, supplying cakes and biscuits to local shops, cafes and catering firms. Here are details of her budget for the months of July, August and September.

Revenue:	July	August	September
Sales	5000	6000	7000
Bank loans	1000	–	–
Government grant		500	
Costs			
Raw materials	1500	2000	2500
Labour	1000	1000	1000
Transport	500	500	500
Heating, lighting etc.	500	500	500
Profit/loss:			

The main sources of cash for Marjorie's Bakery are from sales of her cakes, a bank loan and a one-off government grant.

The main costs for her business are: raw materials such as flour, milk and sugar; labour in the form of staff costs of her baker; power for the oven; and transport to deliver the cakes and biscuits to her customers.

On your own

Study the budget for Marjorie's Bakery and calculate the quarterly totals for her budget. In which month did she make the most profit? Which of her costs are fixed costs? Which are variable costs?

Cashflow problems

Many businesses, like Marjorie's, have to pay for the production of their goods before they receive payment for them. This can cause a cashflow problem. For example, in one month, one of Marjorie's biggest customers was three weeks' late in paying for their order. This meant that Marjorie was short of money with which to pay her staff and her bills, and had to arrange for an overdraft on her bank account.

Cashflow problems can also occur if a customer goes bankrupt and a business has to write off as a bad debt the payment it expected to receive.

For your file

Toni has cashflow problems. What should he do? Should he delay paying his bills with the risk that his suppliers may refuse to supply him in future, or that his electricity supply may be cut off, which would involve re-connection costs? Should he apply to his bank to increase his overdraft, which is already up to its agreed limit? Should he take out a loan with a finance company, which will involve paying a high interest rate on the loan? Or should he borrow the money from friends and agree to share his future profits with them? Write a statement saying what you think Toni should do and explain why.

What is an enterprise challenge?

An enterprise challenge involves working in a team to learn more about the world of business. In this unit, you will be challenged to think of a new business idea, to decide on a business plan and to understand how to make business decisions by running your own business.

In groups

Getting your Big Idea

Imagine you are entering a competition like the BiG Challenge. In your group, suggest as many ideas for a new business as you can, and write them all down on a large sheet of paper. The ideas could be for making things, organising events, selling goods or providing a service.

Be imaginative! Ideas students have come up with in the past include the following:

· A slap-me-awake alarm clock to wake people up for school and work in the morning.

· An i-pod holder made entirely of recycled materials.

· An on-line round-up of sports news to be distributed by e-mail and the Internet.

Aim To understand what an enterprise challenge is and to decide on a new business idea. (Economic wellbeing and financial capability 1.2a, 1.4a, 2.3f, 2.3g, 2.3h, 3g, 4a, 4c, 4f, 4g, 4h)

Makeyourmark Enterprise Challenge

The Makeyourmark Enterprise Challlenge is a national challenge run annually in November. The 2008 challenge was to create an entrepreneurial idea inspired by the Olympic and Paralympic values.

It was won by a team from Waldegrave School for Girls. Their product, 'My little athlete' was like an electronic athlete that could be trained to compete in games. Using Bluetooth, the user can compete with other athletes to see who is the fastest and best!

The BiG Challenge

The BiG Challenge is a competition for budding entrepreneurs in Sheffield schools. Teams of pupils are given £25 cash to start up and run their own business over a six-month period.

Here are some examples of what successful teams have done in the past: selling personalised goods; organising a clothes-swap event; gardening; leaflet delivery; producing a school calendar.

The 2008/9 BiG Challenge overall winners were 9 Peas in a Pod from Fir Vale school. The team of seven Year-10 pupils made and sold jewellery, bags and T-shirts to raise awareness of gun crime.

Spotting a potential market

In order for your business idea to be successful, you need to be able to sell your product or service. That means people have to want to buy it. If there's no demand, it implies you have made something that people do not want. It's no good developing a raspberry and lime drink if nobody likes the taste!

Finding a product or service that people want is known as identifying "a gap in the market."

A raspberry and lime drink – but would people drink it?

In groups

Look at the business ideas that you came up with. Which one do you think most fills a gap in the market? Why? Give reasons for your views.

In pairs

Think about your business idea: Does it have a unique selling point?

Is there anything about your idea that you can change to make it unique? Why is it important to have a unique selling point?

Identifying competitors

You need to identify any competitors in your market. The key question to ask is: 'Is the market big enough for all of us?' In other words:

- **Is demand strong enough for you and your competitors to all exist and make a profit?**
- **Is there some reason why people should buy your product rather than your competitors' products?**

Bear in mind that even if you don't have any competitors when you launch your business, you soon may have. Companies are very good at looking at what their competitors are doing if something is profitable. This may lead to a competitor copying some of your ideas!

The unique selling point

This is what is special about your product – what sets you apart and above all the rest. For example, there are many types of i-pod holder, but the recycled i-pod holders are different, because they are more environmentally friendly. Because most people who buy i-pods are young, and because young people may be more likely to care about the environment, this is a good unique selling point.

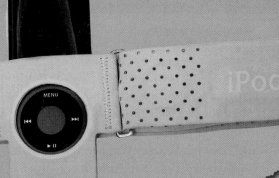

Would you be more likely to buy this i-pod holder or one made from recycled materials?

Making a business plan

Aim To develop a business plan, including a budget plan and a marketing strategy. (Economic wellbeing and financial capability 1.2a, 1.4a, 2.3f, 2.3g, 2.3h, 3g, 4a, 4c, 4f, 4g, 4h)

Making a business plan

Description of your product or service

The first part of your plan should outline what product or service the business offers, its unique selling point and details of who your competitors are and how your business will fill a gap in the market.

To show evidence for the statements you make in this section you will need to have carried out some market research. A common way of doing this is to get people to fill in a questionnaire.

Draft a questionnaire to find out how much of a market there is for the goods or service your business will provide. Give the questionnaire to potential customers. Analyse the results and discuss what they tell you about your proposal. Is there any way you could modify your idea to make it more marketable?

In groups

Think about your business idea. What rate of return do you think you could make? You need to calculate precisely the costs of producing a number of the goods or an amount of the service and how many sales you need in order to generate a satisfactory rate of return.

A budget for the business

Your business plan must contain a detailed budget. This needs to contain information about the start-up costs and running costs, how you are going to finance them, the price you plan to charge for the goods or service, and how you plan to make a profit.

Imagine your school offers you an interest-free loan of £25 towards the start-up costs of your business (repayable from any profits after six months). Discuss whether this is sufficient to meet these costs and how you might raise extra money by getting your friends or family to invest in the business e.g. by selling shares in it.

The price is right?

In order to succeed, your business will need to make a profit. This is when the revenue from your products and services is higher than the costs of making and delivering them.

Profit is important, because it will give you the money to expand your business, to make it successful in the future.

In order to achieve this, you need to make sure that your goods or services are set at the right price, not just so that people can buy them, but so that you can also make a reasonable profit.

Businesses often talk about the rate of return. This is a figure based on how much money you put into the business, and how much you get out over a period of time. For example, if you put £50 into a business, and get £60 back, you make £10 profit. £10 is 20% of £50. So the rate of return is 20%.

Quality versus quantity

You will need to consider how to make sure that as many people buy the product as possible. You will therefore have to decide whether to use high-quality materials, which will make the product better but more expensive, or whether to try to maximise profits by using cheaper materials or offering a more basic service, which may drive demand down.

If you make your product or service too expensive, it might be good, but nobody will buy it. If you make it too cheap, people will be able to afford it, but won't do so unless it is of sufficient quality.

Think about three different goods that you might buy, eg: shoes, music and books. Which do you think is more important – price or quality? Why? Give reasons for your views.

Developing and marketing your product or service

The next section of your plan will give details of how you plan to develop and market your product or service.

If you are developing a product, you will need to consider such things as:

- How and where you are going to obtain any raw materials you require.
- Where and when manufacturing will take place
- The number of goods you will make in your first batch
- How the product will be packaged.

Marketing your product or service

Your business plan should contain details of how you plan to market your product or service.

You need to think about your target customers, and about outlets that might stock and sell your product or make people aware of your service.

Your marketing strategy should outline how you plan to advertise your goods and services. A cheap and effective way of advertising is to produce and distribute a leaflet. As well as delivering it in the neighbourhood, you could make it available in places such as local shops and the community centre.

You might also be able to obtain publicity on the local radio or school radio.

Expanding your business

The business plan should conclude with a brief statement of how you might expand the business, either by re-investing profits or taking out a loan, including details of people and organisations you would approach for advice, such as business advisers and bank managers.

Imagine you have to present your business plan to a panel of judges. You are limited to a five-minute presentation. Take it in turns for groups to present their plans. Then discuss which group has the best business idea. Which group gave the best presentation? How could your group improve its presentation?

Write a short statement saying what you learned from the activities in this unit about the skills and attitudes required for successful teamwork.

22 Reviewing and recording

What you have learned

Aim To review and record what you have learned from studying the units in Your Life 4

How to use this section

- Think about what you have learned in each of the four sections of the course.
- Use the questions below on each section to draft a statement about the knowledge and skills you have developed from studying the units in that section.
- In your statements include any important views, expressing the attitudes and values that you have formed as a result of considering and discussing particular topics.

Here's what Jemma, 15, wrote about what she had learned from the unit on sex and contraception in the 'Keeping healthy' section.

"I learned how important it is to think about sex in the context of a relationship and to discuss things fully with your partner before you have sex. It made me aware of the risks of having unsafe sex and the need to protect yourself by using a condom. Discussing the difficult decisions that you have to face if you get pregnant as a teenager made me realise that I don't believe abortion is right. It made me more determined than ever not to be pressurised into having sex till I feel I'm ready for it."

Section 1   Developing as a citizen

Use these questions to help you to draft a statement about what you learned from this section.

What did you learn…

…about Britain as a diverse society? (Citizenship 1.3a, 1.3b) pages 6–9
- about how the UK developed its diverse national identity, and about how Britain has benefited from ethnic diversity
- about what it means to be British.

…about human rights? (Citizenship 1.2a, 1.2b, 1.2c, 3a) pages 10–13
- about the human rights that underpin society and the responsibility we have to respect other people's rights.

…about rights and responsibilities? (Citizenship 1.2a, 1.2b, 3k) pages 14–19
- about the rights and responsibilities of young people, workers and consumers
- about the legislation that defines responsibilities and protects these rights.

…about the law of the land? (Citizenship 1.1b, 3b, 3c) ages 20–23
- about the different ways in which laws are made
- about the criminal and civil justice systems.

…about crime and punishment? (Citizenship 1.1b, 3b, 3c) pages 24–29
- about the age of criminal responsibility
- about ways of tackling antisocial behaviour and their effectiveness
- about youth crime and the process of youth justice
- about different types of punishment, their aims and their effectiveness.

…about your government? (Citizenship 1.1a, 1.1d, 3c, 3d, 3e) pages 30–35
- about the structure and organisation of Parliament
- about how MPs are elected, and about the importance of voting.

…about your council? (Citizenship 1.1a, 3d) pages 36–41
- about the structure and organisation of local government
- about what devolution is, and how local government is being changed to involve people more in decision-making.

…about working for change? (Citizenship 1.1a, 3d, 3g, 4e) pages 42–47
- about local and national pressure groups
- about how to set up a pressure group and how to mount a campaign in your local area.

Personal wellbeing - Understanding yourself and handling relationships

What have you learned from this section? Use these questions to help you draft a statement.

What did you learn…

… about developing your identity and image? (Personal wellbeing 1.1a, 1.1b, 2.1a) pages 48–49
- about what influences your behaviour
- about your identity and character, and the image you want to convey of yourself
- about what kind of person you want to be.

… about managing your emotions and moods? (Personal wellbeing 1.4a, 1.4c, 2.1d, 2.1e, 2.3a) pages 52–55
- about how to recognise and manage your feelings and moods, and how to deal with disappointment
- about how to behave assertively.

… about changing relationships? (Personal wellbeing 1.4a, 1.4c, 2.1d, 2.1e, 2.3a, 2.3b, 3f, 3g) pages 56–59
- about how to deal with conflict in your

relationship with your parents, and how to deal with pressures on friendships
- about understanding the emotions you experience in close relationships, and what love is.

… about coping with crisis? (Personal wellbeing 2.1d, 2.2a, 2.3e, 3i) pages 60–65
- about the impact of separation, divorce and bereavement on families, and how to adapt to changing circumstances, such as leaving home.

… about challenging offensive behaviour? (Personal wellbeing 1.5a b, 2.1a, 2.3d, 3a, 3j; Citizenship 1.1c, 1.2a, 1.2b) pages 66–69
- about prejudice, racism and religious discrimination, and how to challenge offensive behaviour.

Section 3 **Personal wellbeing – Keeping healthy**

Use these questions to help you to draft a statement about what you learned from this section.

What did you learn…

… about healthy eating? (Personal wellbeing 3b, 3d) pages 70–73
- about attitudes to body image, eating and dieting
- about how to develop healthy eating habits

… about safer sex and contraception? (Personal wellbeing 3d) pages 74–77
- about the risks involved in sexual activity, and what is meant by safer sex
- about different forms of contraception.

… about drinking… (Personal wellbeing 3d) pages 78–79
…and smoking? (Personal wellbeing 3d) pages 80–81
- about the effects of drinking alcohol, and the risks of binge drinking and how to drink sensibly

- about how smoking and passive smoking can damage your health, and how to resist unhelpful pressure to smoke.

… about health matters? (Personal wellbeing 3d, 3e) pages 82–85
- about what you need to know so that you can take responsibility for your own health
- about the risks of sunbathing, tattooing and body piercing.

Section 4 **Economic wellbeing and financial capability**

What have you learned from this section? Use these questions to help you to draft a statement.

What did you learn…

… about planning your future? (Economic wellbeing and financial capability 1.1a b c 1.2c 2.1a b c d 2.2a 2.3a c 3e f 4b) pages 86–91
- about the career and educational opportunities open to you
- about what personal qualities you have and which career paths might be suitable for you
- about work experience.

… about managing your money? (Economic wellbeing and financial capability 1.2b 2.4a b c d 3h) pages 92–95
- about budgeting, bank accounts and saving.

… about financing businesses? (Economic wellbeing and financial capability 1.4a b 3g j 4g) pages 96–101
- about how businesses raise and use money and how to draw up a business budget.

… about developing a business enterprise? (Economic wellbeing and financial capability 1.2a 2.3g h 4c g) pages 102–105
- about creating a new business and developing a business plan.

Index